# ❖ *Remembrances* II ❖

## CHARLES H. NORMAN III

Jan-Carol
Publishing, Inc
"every story needs a book"

*Remembrances II*
Charles H. Norman III

Published February 2024
Heirloom Editions
Imprint of Jan-Carol Publishing, Inc.
All rights reserved
Copyright © 2024 Charles H. Norman III

ISBN: 978-1-962561-15-0
Library of Congress Control Number: 2024930136

You may contact the publisher:
Jan-Carol Publishing, Inc.
PO Box 701
Johnson City, TN 37605
publisher@jancarolpublishing.com
www.jancarolpublishing.com

# PREFACE

To the reader, I thank you for taking the time to read *Remembrances II*. It's a humbling experience knowing that others believe what one might say or write is worthy of taking note. After my thirty-four-year career with the airlines was over, little could I imagine that I'd be writing true-to-life anecdotal short stories and compile them into book form for others to enjoy. This is my second book of this sort, and I'm very honored to share it with you. In life I love telling entertaining, inspirational, challenging stories in person, so I just write like I talk. I think I connect with people that way, and I hope you see that in these stories. Many of these first appeared in *The Glen Rose Reporter*, for which I was a regular Community Guest Columnist for several years. A couple of others appeared in other national publications as noted. Some were freelance and written during the pandemic or written specifically for this book. My goal is to relate to/with you on a personal level about people I've known, places I've been, and experiences I've had, and that it might take you away from the busyness of life for a little while — to challenge, inspire, and entertain you, and to help us appreciate each day we're given by the One who made us all. Happy reading, and I hope you're glad you did!

# TABLE OF CONTENTS

1. Grab Somebody and Just Hold On....................................1

2. Texans Meet Again on Distant Shores.........................5

3. Something In The Way They Wooed Us.....................10

4. Fun Memories from Elementary Days Sports...............14

5. Special Day at The Airport.........................................18

6. Pucker Up, Buddy Boy..............................................22

7. "Doo-Wopper" and Writer Walk Reconciliation Road Together........25

8. Unlikeliest Of Friends................................................30

9. Old Yearbooks Shed Light on High School Romance.........................34

10. Victor in Name — Victor in Life................................38

11. Don't Want to Meat Again.......................................46

12. Too Late in Saying Goodbye....................................50

13. You Don't Know Where the Wind Blows..................56

14. That Was a Shocker Alright!....................................62

15. Starry, Starry Fright.................................................66

16. Elementary Schoolmates Connect............................69

17. Thank God for The Safety........................................73

18.  Remembering My Daddy........................................77

19.  Mommy Might Be Singing a Different Tune.......................80

20.  Famous "Mickey" Was Regular "Mike" To Me.....................84

21.  New Beginnings for Heather....................................87

22.  Catching a "Whopper" at Camp .................................93

23.  From Singer on An Album to Forever Friend....................96

24.  Biology Teacher Had Strange Genes............................101

25.  And The Second Shall Be Last.................................105

26.  Daphne Fay — The Wonder Pug..................................111

27.  One Fine Fellow — True Love Ways.............................114

28.  Gentle Teacher's Gesture Turned Me Around....................119

29.  Respect For a Man of Honor II................................123

30.  Awkward Moments Just a Part of Growing Up....................130

31.  Brothers in More Ways Than One...............................134

32.  Peace Officer On the Police Force............................138

Acknowledgments..................................................145

About the Author.................................................147

# 1

# GRAB SOMEBODY
# AND JUST HOLD ON

The outdoor Christian musical drama *The Promise* is now in the midst of its thirty-five-year run at the 3,000 seat Texas Amphitheater here in Glen Rose. With a cast/crew numbering over a hundred, extraordinary folks from all walks of life sing, dance, and act their way through the Gospel story in the two hours plus production. One can't help but be inspired and challenged by this unique telling of "The Greatest Story Ever Told."

So, it was some twenty-seven years ago when all four members of the Norman clan (me, wife Carolyn, ten-year-old son Charles, and seven-year-old daughter Noelle) were privileged to be a part of *The Promise* family on and off for several years. Our son actually played a major role in helping narrate the story early on in our involvement. Daughter Noelle followed her brother in a similar part a couple years later. Because Charles had a pretty good singing

voice back then — don't ask about now … he's pretty sensitive about that — we were able to ride his coattails into roles ourselves. Well, at least two of us were. Carolyn and Noelle auditioned and were selected for various parts, and I was relegated to ticket-taker/usher. What does that say?

However, somehow fairly early on that first season, I did have my chance to be on stage … at least that *one* time. Seems as if the cast was lacking men to be "crowd's people," and I was recruited from my ushering job to fill in. Duty called. I'm thinking, hey, hey, this could be my chance for the Big-Time! So, I got all dressed "down" for my role of doing nothing but looking like a "beggar man" and milling around in various scenes. *"NO singing, Norman,"* I was told by the producer. One lady/family friend, Pam, was assigned to look after me and just make sure I stayed out of peoples' way and got on and off stage at the proper time. After a scene or two, I started getting the hang of this and began to feel comfortable being out there on stage and in the spotlight. Maybe a little too comfortable…

Okay, here's what happened: it was in the "Baptism at the Jordan River" scene wherein "Jesus" (portrayed by Joel Lagrone) is baptized by "John the Baptist" (portrayed by Allen Conley) and lots of "crowd's people" are participating in and observing the ceremony. I'm out there with my security friend Pam, and we're taking it all in. Then I happened to notice my son Charles (shepherd boy this particular night) across the way holding a baby goat in his arms. I'm

Non-Singing Crowd's Person

thinking that's pretty neat. Maybe I can just meander my way over there, say "Shalom" to my son, pet the goat for a minute or two, and make it back to Pam before the scene is over with plenty of time to exit the stage. I was also told beforehand that if you ever get out there and the scene

2

ends abruptly, and the lights go out, you won't be able to see. Should that happen, just grab ahold of someone, *anyone*, and hang on! They'll lead you offstage — 'cause you definitely don't want to be stuck out there on stage with huge, heavy props being rolled in and out (it's dangerous). Besides, spotlights will be coming on for the next scene within thirty seconds.

Well, you guessed it. The scene ended before I knew it, and Pam was not in sight. In fact, nothing was in sight. I couldn't see anything. Everything went dark! Uh oh … this is not good! So, being the good "fill-in crowd's person" I was, I reached out and grabbed the first person I could get ahold of. It was this guy darting by me very quickly. I grabbed his arm/cloak and I wasn't letting go. I heard him mutter something like, "What are you doing!? Turn me loose! Leave me alone!" But I held on for dear life — "my opportunity as a wannabe star." Next thing I know, this guy sort of hops into an area about the size of a small closet. I follow him … for about five seconds, that is. Let's just say I was quickly shown I did not belong in the quick-change room for "Jesus." His two assistants hoisted me right out of there. They had about forty-five seconds to get him ready for the next scene. Not good again.

By this time, I'm realizing ushering might be my truer calling whether I like it or not. Whatever … But now I gotta go somewhere, and it's dark out there. So, I feel my way around, trying to get off stage. I hear the music start, and man, I'm thinking, "Uh oh, I gotta do something and fast." Being the "smart guy" I am (though I can't seem to find an exit anywhere?), I know if I can get *behind* one of those big twenty by twenty-five-foot stage props, at least the 3,000 people in the audience won't be able to see me. So that's what I did. I felt a little like I was living vicariously in an episode of "I Love Lucy." I hid behind that stage prop for at least for six to seven minutes until the next scene was over … I guess one bonus was, I did get to see "Jesus" from a different perspective.

The thing is, when the show was over, boy, did I lay low. I stayed clear of Joel for a few weeks. Thank the Good Lord, I didn't think Joel actually knew who I was at the time. That was a good thing. But by the end of *The Promise* season that fall, I had gotten to know this fine, quality man who for years portrayed Jesus so well. Joel actually became a family friend, and more importantly, even played a part in helping my own dad come closer to the Lord. So, as *The Promise's* schedule was winding down for the year, I knew I had some confessing to do. I had to tell ol' Joel it was *me* who was hanging onto him that night, hindering his path to the quick-change room. Like the Good Lord himself, Joel already knew, but was just waiting for my confession with a smile and acceptance. There's never a bad time to admit to one's transgressions. I was guilty alright ... and as in real life, forgiveness was just a confession away.

My dad, me, and Joel after *The Promise*

# 2

# TEXANS MEET AGAIN ON DISTANT SHORES

Back in 1975, I was in a new job right out of college and living in Honolulu. What a wonderful opportunity and experience it was for me to do this. I mean, periodically, I'd just stop and gaze around and take in the lush view of the mountains of Manoa Valley, walk the glistening sands of Waikiki Beach, and peer out at the vast Pacific Ocean disappearing on the horizon. A far cry from the arid plains of West Texas and my hometown of Odessa, some 3,500 miles to the east. In a way, I sort of wondered how I got there.

While there for about three years, I volunteered as a Big Brother in the Big Brother Organization. One evening I took my "little brother" David to a showing of an amateur Underwater Film Festival at one of the local high schools. I'd done a little scuba diving since getting certified and thought little David might enjoy the films. So, there we were, the two of us in this auditorium full of about 400 – 500 underwater enthusiasts when I just glanced around and happened to notice this one gal who caught my eye for some reason. Not only was she quite pretty, but my goodness, she sure looked like someone I used to know from my days way back at Crockett Junior High and Odessa High. But that'd been seven or eight years ago since I would have last seen Donna; and if it was her, what in the world would she be doing in Hawaii!?

The film clips of scuba diving in Hawaii were entertaining alright, and my little David did enjoy them, but I couldn't get this possible encounter with an old classmate out of my mind. So as the movies ended, with little David in tow, I maneuvered my way quickly toward this young lady to be able to at least say "hello." When I got within earshot of her, I simply said, "Excuse me, do you happen to be from Texas?"

"Charlie, it *is* you!" It was Donna ... and her husband Dave who was stationed in the Navy there. Dave was also from Odessa, although I did not know him. They were both one year my junior in school. We caught up ever so briefly and exchanged phone numbers.

I knew in my heart this was a divine appointment. Now, I was a relatively new Christian of about three years at the time, but I was also beginning to understand this is sometimes how the Lord works — by orchestrating events, timing of circumstances, and people meeting (again?) for the greater good and His purposes. I had no sense one way or another of where Dave and Donna stood spiritually. I just knew they were fellow Texans, they seemed like good people, and I wanted to get to know them. We had Odessa and Hawaii in common. Not too many folks can say that!

So, a couple weeks later, I took my close friend and fellow church member Denise with me out to meet Donna and Dave at their home at the Navy Base to get reacquainted and hopefully share our experiences on how we individually came to know the Lord. Denise was formerly a nun in New York, and I knew she had a whole 'nother wonderful kind of testimony. Donna and Dave were so nice and hospitable, and they had the cutest little boy, six-year-old Johnny. After a time of catching up, reminiscing, and sharing fun anecdotes, they were attentive to our testimonies, which seemed to flow naturally and easily. We visited about an hour, and then as we left, I handed Donna an album recorded by an Odessan and fellow school choir member of hers from back in the day. On the album Jerry sang, played guitar, and spoke about *his* new life in Christ. I found out later that Donna and Dave thought we were both "crazy." But Denise and I prayed that hopefully we had at least planted a spiritual seed in their hearts. They were good people for sure but needed a deeper, committed personal relationship with the One who made them.

With our faith sharing, along with some other Christian friends of theirs in the Navy, a stirring had begun in their souls. Unbeknownst to me, they were also struggling somewhat financially at the time. They needed some $400 for a payment that was due within three days of our visit, and they only had a little over $100 in the bank. For some reason, Donna decided, "Okay, if what all these people are saying is true, why don't we just put the Lord to a test — a 'fleece' if you will." With Dave's okay, they gave all the monies they had in the bank to a needy cause there at the base, all the time wondering if this was really the right thing to do. Two days later, they found an anonymous envelope in their mailbox with exactly the $400 they needed for their payment ... hmm.

A few days after that, Donna appeared at my workplace unannounced with album in hand. She seemed strangely subdued as she gave the record back to me, and all she said was "thank you" as she turned and walked away. Two days later I received a phone call from Donna, and I heard the words any true believer longs to hear: "Charlie, I accepted Jesus into my life last night." I was so thrilled, touched, and humbled, I was speechless. To have been a part of this life-changing decision for my sweet friend Donna was such an honor. I then asked, "How's Dave?" She said, "Well, he's not quite there yet, but I feel it's just a matter of time." A few days later, sure enough I got another phone call, this time from Dave, and he told me of his decision to follow Christ as well. What wonderful news!

I asked him how that all came about. He said he was talking on the phone with this Christian friend of his, when this friend just flat-out asked him if he'd like to pray with him to receive Christ. He said "Yes," so right then and there, on the phone, in prayer and in his underwear, he became a part of the family of God. The Bible tells us angels in Heaven were rejoicing.

For the next year or so, I'd get to see Dave and Donna around and observe the wonderful transformation taking place in their lives. I was witnessing what God had wrought. They got involved in a good Bible-believing church and found their calling in Child Evangelism. Within a couple of years, they adopted two Korean baby girls, Becky and Tina, to complete their family, and be sisters to little Johnny.

Dave and I grew closer as brothers in Christ and did a few scuba dives together. The best dive I ever had was with Dave out at Hanauma Bay on Oahu's eastern shore. It was just me and him down about seventy-five feet when he speared a sea urchin and cut it into pieces. Within seconds we were surrounded by swarms fish of all makes and colors. It was like flashes of brilliant rainbow prisms darting in and around us, nudging us as they swam past. I never ever forgot that moment in time. Dave commented to me afterwards that ever since Jesus came into his life, it just seems all the colors of things he once used to take for granted are now so much brighter and more vivid than ever before. Yeah, I thought so, too. The Lord has a way of doing that.

I left Hawaii about a year later for a new job, and Dave and Donna moved back to the mainland after his stint with the Navy. But we stayed in touch and eventually we all ended up back in Texas — God's country — and close enough that we could still see each other on occasion. Over the years though, Donna developed some serious health issues, yet her faith in the Lord Jesus never wavered.

My dad passed away in September 2007 at age eighty-five. I recall my friend Dave calling me that very week and telling me his fifty-six-year-old wife Donna had just joined my dad in Heaven. So sad for us, but oh so happy for them. No more suffering. Only peace and joy.

Within a couple of years, Dave did remarry. The Lord had brought a Christian lady named Carla back into his life — someone he had known forty years earlier in Odessa. It was good, and right, and beautiful. I attended their garden wedding at a very nice home in North Dallas. At the end of the ceremony, one of Dave's (and Donna's) grown daughters, Becky, sought me out, came right up to me, and said these words I'll never forget: "Charlie, my mother is in Heaven because of you." I was so humbled… I hardly knew what to say. This was probably the greatest honor I could ever receive.

P.S. My good friend and Brother Dave is now not in the best of health himself. He's losing his eyesight to macular degeneration, and in the not-too-distant future will be unable to see much of anything. I think about our time together on occasion — seeing all those shining, colorful fish swarming all about us in the clear, blue waters of Hawaii. He and I will never experience that again. But Dave has kept his eye on the prize. And because we know our Creator, the One who made the heavens and the earth, we can look forward to that glorious day when our eyes are opened to sights unimaginable, wonders unfathomable, and glimmering radiant colors we know not of. All because of a life transformed by Jesus and His promise of life everlasting.

P.S.S. About three years ago, at Dave's seventieth birthday party in East Texas, his daughter Becky came up to introduce me to her two young teenage girls, saying, "Charlie, I'd like you to meet my daughters, Grace and Faith. They're believers, too. Your legacy lives on, my brother. Thank you." Humbled and speechless again, I could only give thanks to the One who orchestrated it all and knew us from the womb.

At Dave's 70th birthday party

# 3

# SOMETHING IN THE WAY THEY WOOED US

Like seventy-three million other television viewers on Sunday night, February 9, 1964, little did we know we were witnessing history in the making. It was then that TV host Ed Sullivan introduced for the very first time The Beatles to the USA on his weekly variety show. Our country had been in long solemn mourning since President Kennedy's assassination two and one-half months earlier, and we could scarcely imagine it would be four young guys from Liverpool, England, that would catapult us from a national collective funk into a new era of music, culture, hope, and optimism.

With Ed's introduction, "Now, ladies and gentlemen, The Beatles!" it was as if the palpable excitement in the theater itself was also somehow being transmitted to American living rooms from coast to coast. Starting with the television close up of doe-eyed Paul McCartney singing "Close your eyes and I'll kiss you … tomorrow I'll miss you," The Beatles were captivating an unsuspecting audience of millions of young (and not-so-young) people across our land. Count me in. As a slightly naïve, impressionable thirteen-year-old youngster from the arid plains of West Texas, I didn't quite know what to make of this new kind of music emanating from this quartet of British musicians. But whatever it was, I *LIKED* it. There was an edgy innocence, a driving backbeat, and a youthful exuberance that somehow shook our nation's somber psyche and had us believing in ourselves again. Smiles were returning to the faces. Moreover, it was not only their distinctive, upbeat sound, but it was their stage presence and their look that wooed a country. They had the *"IT"* factor before we even knew what *IT* was.

With their sharp, matching collarless suits/ties (remember Beatle boots, anyone?) to their longer, yet clean-cut hairstyle, John, Paul, George, and Ringo proceeded to serenade the largest audience in the history of television. The United States was ripe to be smitten, and smitten we were. When the Beatles performed their second number — a throwback version of the hit "Till There Was You" from the Broadway musical "The Music Man," even parents, grandparents, and older folks had to admit that these lads obviously had talent, originality, and a different kind of attraction that was hard to explain.

So, it was from that auspicious beginning on Ed Sullivan's show that The Beatles became the mainstay of American pop culture for the rest of the decade and far beyond. I knew that Beatle music had attained "legitimacy" when our ballroom dance instructors put on a 45-rpm single of "I Saw Her Standing There" and we learned new steps to the "jitterbug." With its unmistakable vocal count-in of 1-2-3-4, that

Charlie (2nd from left) on his seventh birthday, July 6, 1957. The *very same day*, John Lennon and Paul McCartney met for the first time at a church fete in Liverpool, England.

song became an instant classic and quite the rocker to get one's body and feet a-movin'! This sound had become *my* generation's music. I had found my ticket to ride. How exciting it was to hear a new Beatles song on the radio for the first time! To this day, I can remember when and where I was when I first heard that penetrating opening chord of "A Hard Day's Night," the soft solo acoustic guitar melody of "Yesterday," and the unique feedback/reverb on the first few seconds of "I Feel Fine." Whenever a new Beatles song came out, it seemed the music just exuded an energy and positiveness that was infectious, and it made you feel happy and hopeful no matter. Whether you made a poor grade on a quiz in school, or you were going through the uncertainty of a budding adolescence romance, or your favorite team had just lost an important ball game to your arch rival, all we had to do was sing along with The Beatles when they shouted, "Don't you know it's gonna be … all right! all right! all right!" And then we felt that soon, somehow, things would be getting better.

Yes, there were things about The Beatles (especially in the later years involving politics, philosophy, etc.) that I did not agree with or endorse, but I made a decision. I consciously chose to embrace the happier, more innocent songs, to appreciate the tight harmonies and sweet melodies, and to savor the uplifting exuberant sound The Beatles brought to my world from adolescence to my time now as a grandfather. The harmony and melodies of so many of these early songs have stayed with me all these years. In the early 2000s, I introduced my own two pubescent kids to The Beatles, and they too got the bug and became avid fans.

A few years later I was able to secure four tickets for the family to go see Paul McCartney in concert in Dallas. What a thrill it was to see this icon, this influential man from my past, right before my eyes, crooning ever so believably once again, "All my troubles seemed so far away!" It was a surreal moment in time for me … recalling some forty years earlier that black and white visual image of Paul sitting on a stool all alone with acoustic guitar in hand singing "Yesterday" on Ed Sullivan in what was to become the most-covered song of all-time in the history of music. But you know what was even more special for me than all that? It was to be with my wife, teenage son and daughter, and 18,000 other joyous souls, joining Sir Paul in belting out "Twist and Shout" while dancing in the aisles. It does not get any better than this. Yes, back in 1964, there was music all around, but I never really heard it at all… "Till There Was…The Beatles!" Yeah, Yeah, Yeah.

*This article was originally published in:* Good Old Days Magazine, *July/Aug 2020, goodolddaysmagazine.com and reprinted by permission.*

## *4*

# FUN MEMORIES FROM ELEMENTARY DAYS SPORTS

Sports played a big part of my growing-up days out in Odessa. I mean, we didn't have trails to hike, lakes to fish, or mountains to climb. But even in elementary school, we had teams — football, basketball, track, and baseball, in that order. Because I participated in each of those sports, I have memories that have stuck with me all these years.

I loved and felt proud to represent Austin Elementary School — home of the Fightin' Blue and Gold. In football, I was put in at the quarterback position by Coach Tommie Harrison. Played second team behind my friend Bryce — a taller, stronger, more talented athlete than me. I say, I "played." Well, truth be known, on a good game day, I might get on the field five-six-seven minutes and get to run a couple of series. I will say, though, I did complete 100% of my passes over the course of the season! Yep, all four of 'em were

That's me circled...only player whose jersey number does not show. Go figure. Ha! (circa 1961)

thrown to and caught by my friend Terry. So there! You see, *I wanted to be Bryce* 'cause he played almost the entire game and could call/throw as many passes as he wanted.

Fast forward some fifty-five years later, and Bryce and I reconnected and had lunch together in Fort Worth one fine day. We enjoyed reliving some of those times from our school days, and I finally fessed up and told him of my envy of his days playing QB when we were sixth graders ... you know, calling his own plays and getting to throw all those passes in the games we played. He then said to me: "Charlie, wanna know how many passes I threw that year?" He paused, then said "Zero. ZERO! I *never* called a pass the whole time I played QB at Austin." Well, after that revelation, *I no longer wanted to be Bryce.* So there! Ha!

Now basketball was a little different, because I was good enough to start for my team. Scored a few points, too. One game I was top scorer (four points ... hey, hey!) and my favorite girlfriend Katrina came to watch me play. We won and I got to hold her hand as we took a five-minute walk around the schoolyard after the victory. All that was quite short-lived though. Not sure we won many more games after that, and Katrina decided for some reason she liked an upperclassman, a sixth-grader named Arnold, better than me. Bummer. Go figure. Our basketball team was mediocre at best, and I think the last game we won was because some kid on San Jacinto's team scored two points for us by making a goal on the *wrong end* of the court. I felt a little sorry for the guy because that could have very easily been me. But hey, a win's a win, and we'll take it!

Then on to track where I competed in the fifty-yard dash, the high jump, and 440 relay. I got "smoked" by a little kid from Carver Elementary in the fifty-

Austin's 1st trophy in decades

15

yard dash, but did manage to win the high jump event with a jump of about four feet, with my wheelchair-bound granddad looking on. We also won the relay and took home the first trophy Austin Elementary had snared in over a decade. A few decades later, *that very trophy* was given to me by the school principal when the school was doing some renovations, and old trophies were relegated to the basement.

Then it was on to baseball, where I played second base. I wasn't much of a hitter, but I could field the ball pretty good. One game in particular I remember, we were playing Burnet — that uppity school from the east side of town, all decked out in their spiffy red and black uniforms. I was jealous of how classy those uniforms looked compared to our old faded blue and gold T-shirts. The thing was, our pitcher, Manuel, was struggling, and we couldn't seem to get their team out. They were hitting him like he was tossing the ball underhand. Those kids from Burnet were scoring ten to fifteen runs per inning — back then the rules didn't mandate a maximum number of runs allowed per inning. I distinctly recall standing out there near second base, and just started crying. Really crying. I was embarrassed and humiliated for Austin and my teammates. Big-time tears for a little kid. Finally, Coach Harrison turned to me and asked if I wanted to try my "arm" at pitching. Well, why not? I did and got the last two outs for our team. That was the *only time I ever pitched* in a game anytime. I think we probably lost something like 43 – 5, but I did try my best, and it was a learning, humbling experience for me for sure. It was just a

Me and Coach Harrison
(circa 1961)

game that nobody remembers — except me.

P.S. That kid from the San Jacinto team that scored the winning basket for my team by mistake? Come to find out, just a couple of years ago, that kid's name is Steve, and one of my closest friends now — some sixty years later! Of all things, and much to his chagrin, we were the ones playing against each other in that game. He was hoping nobody would ever remember his scoring that basket for the opposing team. Not me. I did. No wonder I like this guy so much!

Steve McCleery and me —
60 years later in Lubbock, Texas

# 5

# SPECIAL DAY
# AT THE AIRPORT

For several years after I retired from my job with the airline, I'd drive up to DFW and do some volunteer work. I'd be all dressed up in my old airline uniform, wearing my old ID badge, and carrying a clipboard for notes/numbers/airport diagrams for reference. I'd go up there every week or two and make a day of it by roaming the concourses looking for folks who might need a hand — helping them find their next flight, carrying an extra piece of luggage, or assisting an elderly person maneuver the crowds. I'd usually make twenty-five to thirty personal contacts on behalf of my former employer each time I went, and I felt especially useful many a day. Sometimes, I just knew I was meant to be there.

Timing is everything, and so it was on this special day. I'd been there about six hours and was actually on my way toward the exit in Terminal D when I passed the big "Arrivals/Departures" monitor near Gate 40. I then noticed one lone twenty-something woman peering up at the screen. She looked a little confused and concerned, so I stopped and asked if I could help. She was of Asian descent and spoke no English but pointed up at the screen. I figured she was looking for her connecting flight. I asked/motioned for her to show me her ticket and she readily complied. I saw from her ticket that her destination was Seoul, Korea, and that she had just flown in from Uruguay to catch a connecting flight at DFW. The thing is, I was also aware there was only one flight per day to Seoul, and it had left a couple hours earlier. Not good. I spoke no Korean (assuming that was her language), but I knew where to go for the International Help Desk, not too far away, for some assistance.

So, I got the lady I'll call "Binna" to follow me. We got to the counter, and I began to intervene on her behalf and explain the situation to the agent (who did speak Korean) and who was immediately sympathetic. Sure enough, Binna was on a delayed fight out of Uruguay and, therefore, missed her connecting flight on from DFW. She was on her way to her *wedding* in Korea — two days away! She had no cell phone, no US money, no place to go, and the next flight to get her to Seoul was the following afternoon. The agent and I came up with a plan for Binna. She got rebooked for the flight the next day (First Class, no less), and we used my cell phone to call a relative in California to explain what happened, who in turn, was able relay the information to her family in Korea. Because it was no fault of her own for the delay in Uruguay (airline mechanical), it was protocol to secure a hotel, transportation, and meal voucher for the inconvenienced customer. That got all settled (with next day's boarding pass in hand), and we made arrangements with the hotel for her to be able to send an email to her family explaining things more fully. The agent went over everything again — when and where for hotel pick up, ticketing, vouchers, etc.

Knowing Binna would probably appreciate an escort outside "Security" to catch her van ride to her hotel, and into a world she knew not of, I became that escort. As we waited outside by the curb, I could tell Binna was going to be okay. The hotel van appeared, and I was able to briefly communicate with the driver her situation. He assured me Binna was in good hands. I opened the door for her to get in, then Binna looked at me with tears in her eyes. Then she gave me the sweetest hug of gratitude I could ever imagine. Though we spoke different languages, we had connected as humans with kindred spirits. She had a need, and I was there to help. It was a great privilege to be used that way that day. As the van drove her off, we waved goodbye, and I, too, had tears.

So, I start walking toward my car in the parking garage when I spotted a middle-aged gentleman standing by his van near the curb looking a little distraught. I asked him if something was wrong. In his European accent, he asked if I would mind watching his vehicle for just a very few minutes (four or five?), while he took his two large bags for check-in at the counter right inside for his flight to Frankfurt. I knew this is not airline protocol and could be a security issue. The man explained further that his vehicle was a rental and he needed to take it to the South Remote Parking area to turn it in, and he did not want to lug his two large bags on/off a courtesy shuttle. It could be quite cumbersome. I've been there. I got it. I glanced around and saw the Lufthansa counter inside with no one in line. Oh, why not? I mean, if parking patrol comes by, I'll try to be his advocate. "Okay, make it quick." "Oh yes, yes! Thank you, thank you!" He pulled these two huge suitcases out of the van and high-tailed to the counter about fifty feet inside. I dutifully watched his van, no cops came by, and four minutes later my new German acquaintance came hustling out. The deed was done. All good. He started thanking me again and again. I told him it was my privilege. He then noticed my tie (an American Flag design) and said, "I love your tie! And I love the United States of America! How blessed you are to call this place home!" It

Proud to be
an American!

took me back a bit and reminded me once again to not take my wonderful country for granted. He shook my hand in genuine gratitude; and as he drove off, the words just came as I sang softly to myself *"God bless America, land that I love"*... and the tears started flowing once again.

# 6

# PUCKER UP, BUDDY BOY

A few years ago, I got reacquainted with an old schoolmate of mine from Odessa, a fellow I had not seen in some fifty years. Howard was a successful business man in Fort Worth, and though he was a couple years younger than me and I did not know him well back then, it was easy to connect over lunch about our school days and times at Odessa High.

Funny thing, I actually do have a somewhat awkward and "funny-now, not-so-funny then" tale involving Howard that *he* remembered all too well. Back in the day, our school sponsored an annual spring "Sadie Hawkins Week," wherein the girls would invite the boys out for dates, dinner, and the dance. As a senior about to graduate, I claimed no special gal at the time. So, one brave sophomore girl, "Brenda" (bless her heart), invited me out to be her date. Now Brenda was cute, sweet, and a really fun girl alright, but I don't know … she was two years younger than me; I was headed off to college in a few months and just didn't have that spark toward her that maybe she did for me. But she really wanted me to go out and nobody else asked, so I thought "Well, why not?" She'd arrange everything.

So, the big night came, and she was at my door right on time. I stepped out of my house, and there was *Howard* and his date in his car waiting for us in my driveway. I did not know we were double dating, but on further thought I'm thinking this might be a good thing. A foursome might make the evening even more enjoyable. So, Brenda and I climbed into the back-seat and we were off for hamburgers and cokes, and then on to the dance. We actually did have a fun evening, and I was glad I went. It was good to have Howard and his date along for the company and conversation. *Then it dawned on me* — when we get back to my house, Brenda's going to walk me to the door and probably expect a *kiss*. Uh oh… You see, I hadn't had much experience in those things (I don't think that awkward buss on Sharon's elbow in the 1st grade counts). So, on the drive home, I started to dread what I thought might be coming. I didn't want to hurt Brenda's feelings or embarrass myself, and she really was a sweet girl, so I decided I'd just give her a nice big ol' "thank-you" hug. Yeah, that'll work. Not.

We pulled up in my driveway — of course my parents *would* have the porch light on — when Howard just blurted out, "Well, Charlie, guess it's about time for you and Brenda to have that goodnight kiss, wouldn't you say?" What? *Oh No!* Not only am I now feeling obliged, but in front of two witnesses to boot! This was not good. I just knew they'd be peering from the front seat of the car to view the action (or nonaction) about to take place. I was trapped. So, as we walked to the door, I told Brenda I did have a good time, thanked her for the evening, and then I guess I gave her a quick bun-gling peck of a kiss somewhere on the face. I don't remember how it felt or much else, except I did feel sorry for Brenda. I'm sure I was a disappoint-ment to her. Surely in my clumsiness, it was not what she expected.

Well, fast forward some fifty years later, and I'm with wife Carolyn in Nashville for her forty-fifth high school reunion. We're tooling around town, and she's showing me some of her old haunts from long ago. She drove me by one of the houses where she used to live and stopped the car to reminisce a moment. Then she said, "See that front porch there? That's where I had my first-ever kiss." Her remembrance and mention of it actually propelled me back to 1968 and my own bumbling, humbling experience. I didn't know quite what to say or how to react. Then, being the "mature human being" I purport to be, and husband of Carolyn for forty years, I just smiled and smugly said "Well, sweet wife, I hope your first was a lot better than mine." Ha!

P.S. You know, back in those days, it must have taken a lot of courage for a sophomore girl to ask a senior guy out for a date. So, "Brenda" if you're out there somewhere and happen on this article, do know I knew there were better days/dates to come for you. Awkward as it was, thanks for fond remembrances and giving me something fun to write about!

Site of Carolyn's first    Sealing the deal 14 years later    Site of Charlie's bungle

# 7

# "DOO-WOPPER" AND WRITER WALK RECONCILIATION ROAD TOGETHER

It wasn't something I planned. It all started in September 2020 when I heard a song on ol' Pat Boone's Oldies Radio Show on Sirius XM. The song was "Tonight Could Be the Night" by a group called *The Velvets* from my old hometown of Odessa in 1961 — one of the first-ever "Doo-Wop" groups of the genre. The thing is, I grew up in Odessa and had never heard of them before. Though they had several songs that made the national music charts in the early '60s, only a few of the old timers knew of The Velvets, and those that did, were from The Southside ... the Black Community in town.

Being a short story writer, I started to do some research and became fascinated with the narrative. The Velvets were made up of five guys — an 8th grade English teacher and four students from their school, Blackshear Junior/Senior High School. Their music was known for its tight harmonies, vocal clarity, and an infectious, exuberant kind of sound that would lift the spirits of anyone within earshot. They became one of the country's premiere "Doo-Wop" singing groups and recorded some thirty songs over a period from 1961 - 1964, including a #1 hit in Japan "Lana" in August 1961. All that being said, they were basically unacknowledged by the people who lived just on the *other* side of the tracks. *That* was fixin' to change. *That became my calling.*

Finding out that two of the five guys were still around (and that one, Mark Prince, the bass singer, lived in nearby Fort Worth), I reached out to Mark in the hopes of writing a short story about the group. So, I drove up to meet Mark in great anticipation of what he was going to share with me … all the while not knowing he was about to tell me things — deep, heavy things I knew not of.

The timing of this first encounter was right after the summer of George Floyd. With racial tensions in our country running so high, I didn't really know what to expect. But seventy-eight-year-old Mark was more than hospitable to me, and we connected right away. We talked for over two hours, and he told me all about how the group got started … and how *he* got started as a young singer — just singing along with his dad's old Duke Ellington and Count Basey records. He told me what fun it was to get to know Roy Orbison (the up-and-coming music star from the area) and how Roy became the group's link to record producer Fred Foster and Monument Records in Nashville.

Though Mark was about eight years older than me, we conversed easily about our growin'-up time in Odessa. We enjoyed reminiscing about our common favorite places to eat and other things we liked to do. Our conversation ran the gamut — from the Dallas Cowboys and favorite TV shows/movies, to running track for our schools and the special teachers that meant so much to us. You name it, we talked about it. The Good Lord quickly and easily became a part of our conversation and the spiritual bond we had in Him.

I also learned that Jim Crow not only lived in Little Rock, Birmingham, and Greensboro, but also in our isolated hometown in West Texas. I was totally unaware of this. Just plain ignorant I was. Though before my time, I was still embarrassed and ashamed when he told me of certain places he was denied entry into (certain eateries, theaters, clothing stores, etc.) because of the color of his skin. I knew of these places because I went there … freely. Never knew of any discrimination or bigotry. Surely not in Odessa!? But Mark would mention these things only when I probed. He wasn't bitter. He was better than that. He told me that his parents and pastor taught him to replace the discrimination he experienced with acceptance, the rejection with forgiveness, and the hate with love. No room in his heart for the bad stuff, he told me. Towards the end of that first two-hour meeting, he looked at me straight on and set me on my calling for the next two years with these words: "Charlie, *I love you* as my brother."

So, there I was, just seeking out a story-line for an article in *The Glen Rose Reporter*, my little town's weekly newspaper — and I left with the thought of doing a book. I had garnered enough information in that short time with Mark that I couldn't wait to process what he'd told me and then go back for more. I called my publisher, told her of my encounter and conversation with Mark, and she said, "Every story deserves a book, and this is a story that needs to be told! I'll help you." The book *ROAD TO RECON-*

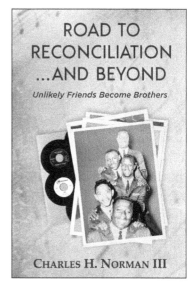

*CILIATION … AND BEYOND Unlikely Friends Become Brothers* (Jan-Carol Publishing 2022) is a product of that encounter and subsequent meetings with Mark.

The book became the catalyst for what in two years' time became known as *The Velvets Endeavor* during Juneteenth Celebration week in Odessa, June 2022. Through countless phone calls, meetings, interviews, zoom calls, and trips to Odessa, a group of several former 1968 Odessa

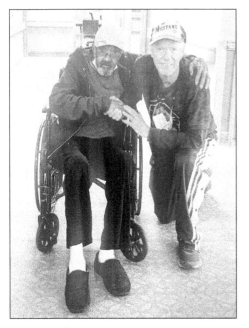

Brothers and friends

High School graduates caught the vision of having some type of belated recognition ceremony and community gathering in Odessa. Its purpose would be to finally acknowledge and properly recognize The Velvets for their immense talent and cultural contribution to the fair city of Odessa and to bring people across racial and generational lines together in a demonstration of *community unity*, regardless of hue of skin. This did happen. Various civic leaders, the Odessa Chamber of Commerce, the Black Chamber of Commerce, the Heritage of Odessa Foundation, the Black Cultural Council of Odessa, the Mayor's office, and the Ector County Independent School District officials all joined in this significant celebration in the very auditorium where The Velvets first practiced and performed back in 1960. Though my friend Mark had since passed away (November 2021), he knew of the planning for this event. We even had a Mayor's Proclamation of June 18, 2022, as *Velvet's Day* across the city, and the dedication of a Historical Marker to the Velvets unveiled just outside the auditorium itself. Miss Frizella Whitiker (ninety-three-years-young retired English teacher and Matriarch of the Black Community) and Robert Earl Thursby (from Hawaii and the last surviving member of The Velvets) were special guests of honor. There was a "Make A New Friend Today" Reception after the program. What a time of healing, celebration, community unity, and acceptance was wrought that glorious day, and in days since! What a privilege to be part something that you know the Good Lord Himself put you on! This was my calling and my honor.

*To read of the full story of how it all began and the positive effects of The Velvets Endeavor you can order:* ROAD TO RECONCILIATION … AND BEYOND Unlikely Friends Become Brothers *from Jan-Carol Publishing directly at (423) 926-9983 or at Amazon.com or Barnesandnoble.com.*

**To view videos of the Velvets/Velvets Endeavor montages go to:**
- DRB Media Communications — The Velvets
- ECISD — Remembering The Velvets (awarded 2 silver tellys)
- VELVETS "Tonight" Video montage: vimeo.com/671545494/5294db09f9
- "Growin' Up Blackshear" Video montage: vimeo.com/684389140

## 8

# UNLIKELIEST OF FRIENDS

For the first eighteen years of my life, I grew up and lived in the fair West Texas town of Odessa. Yeah, I know — flat, arid, brown, windy, few trees, blue collar, the Oil Patch. But there's a lot of good folks out there. I got a solid education; and those Western sky sunsets are often so spectacular, it makes even the busiest of people stop and take notice. The thing is though, just a couple miles away from where I grew up, there was a whole 'nother world I hardly knew existed. It was known as the Southside — the BLACK Community from across the railroad tracks. Seems I might have gone over there two or three times in all my years … for an elementary school track meet circa 1961? I guess the thinking was, they've got their lives over there, and we've got ours over here. Little did I know that when Black folks *did* come over to our side of town in the '50s and '60s (for work mainly — menial jobs, labor, helpers, house cleaners), they'd often encounter Jim Crow and his ilk, and the discriminatory policies/ways from my side of town. No need to stir the pot, you see. I was too young to know any different, and it was surely not my concern.

I was really ignorant of all this until I met seventy-eight-year-old former fellow Odessan Mark Prince in 2020, who at the time lived in North Fort

Worth. Mark happened to be the bass singer of one of the first-ever "Doo Wop" genre singing groups — *The Velvets,* from back in the early '60s. The group consisted of Mark, his 8th grade English teacher Mr. Virgil Johnson (lead singer), and three of Mark's classmates. And yes, they were all from Odessa and the Southside. And man, oh man, could they sing! The Velvets actually had several songs that made the national music charts, including the #1 hit "Lana" in Japan in the summer of 1961. Ironically, The Velvets were better known nationwide than they were in their hometown of Odessa. What a shame to realize this gifted recording group was not properly recognized or honored in their own hometown ... and that sang volumes to me.

As I was doing research about The Velvets for a short story (I thought), I got to talking to Mark about his life growing up in Odessa, and he told me about a number of terrific teachers that greatly influenced him. When probed a little more, there was one particular teacher that came to mind — his high school English teacher, Miss Frizella Whitiker. What a profound positive impact she had had on him and countless others. And *she's still around!* ... ninety-four years young now, Miss Whitiker lives right across

Miss Frizella C. Whitiker

the street from the school where she taught Junior and Senior English for decades to every student who ever graduated from Blackshear High School. Mark told me she was a disciplinarian of the first degree, but that *everyone* came to love and respect Miss Whitiker — because they knew she loved them. Tough love. She knew her calling in life was to prepare her students for the cold world they'd soon be facing outside the halls of Blackshear High. And she did. Not only academically, but in wisdom dealing with life's uncertainties, challenges, and unfairnesses, did she impart insight to those who would listen to the realities coming their way. She also planted spiritual seeds in their hearts — that the true path to joy, direction, and peace in life is being at peace with their Maker ... living that life as a witness to her students.

When talking with Mark, the thought came to me that if there's any way I could somehow meet this lady, this Matriarch of The Southside, I knew I could glean some historical and cultural insight into a world unknown to me until just recently. What a privilege that would be! That meeting did happen. Initially, just over the phone, we got to talk. Right off, I could tell this wise lady was someone special. Born in 1929 in Greenwood, Louisiana, she got her teaching degree at Huston-Tillotson College in Austin and shortly thereafter moved to Odessa in 1950 (the same year I was born), where she taught Junior and Senior English at Blackshear until its closing in 1966. She then moved down the road a couple of miles to Ector High School, where she continued to teach for a number of years.

Mark said that she did not put up with any shenanigans, but kids respected her because they could tell she cared — *really cared* — for her students. Mark said it was like Miss Whitiker had these nuggets of wisdom and experiences in her mind that she wanted to convey to her students, preparing them for the days beyond schooling. Never married, Miss Whitiker would claim these thousands of students as *her* family. She loved them and her school dearly (she wrote the lyrics to the Blackshear school song). Though the school was repurposed many years ago as a magnet elementary school, the original Blackshear auditorium

Charlie and Miss Whitiker
at Velvets Endeavor (June 2022)

was refurbished a few years back and renamed the Frizella C. Whitiker Auditorium at a dedication service in 2021. Her legacy continues.

As I was writing my book about The Velvets — *ROAD TO RECONCILIATION … AND BEYOND* — I had the privilege of meeting Miss Whitiker several times and telling her the story of my purpose in writing the book. She was very much an encouragement to me. She'd say things like: "You're on the right track. You keep writing." "I think it's marvelous that you're reaching out to the Black Community the way you are." "It's very commendable in trying to build these bridges among all people." So that's what I did. Miss Whitiker was an exhorter to me, an inspirer. We've become friends, and with our common faith in the Good Lord, we've grown to love one another as brother and sister, just as the Good Book says: Thou Shalt Love Thy Neighbor as Thyself. Who could ever have imagined this scenario some six decades ago — a seventy-three-year-old White man who left Odessa in 1968, developing a loving friendship with a Black lady of kindred spirit who lives some 300 miles away? We know WHO. We even talked about Heaven a little bit, and I told her *my* mother will surely be in the welcoming party at her homecoming when the day comes (ask for "Minnie Fay"), and they would really like each other. We're family, and that's how He works.

P.S. I distinctly remember my first phone conversation with Miss Whitiker. We were talking about the sad, divisive state of affairs in our country (this was the summer of 2020 after the George Floyd incident). She mentioned a song from the '60s that epitomizes the sentiment we both were feeling: "What the World Needs Now Is Love, Sweet Love." Miss Whitiker lives out that sentiment every day.

# 9

# OLD YEARBOOKS SHED LIGHT ON HIGH SCHOOL ROMANCE

A few weeks ago, I came across my parents' old Odessa High School yearbooks from back in 1938, 1939, and 1940. From letters, notes, and writings in their yearbooks by fellow students, I gained a deeper insight into my folks' relationship in their early years together. I also got a better picture of what life must have been like as a high schooler in West Texas in the years just preceding WWII. I knew some, from stories that my parents had shared with me growing up, but now I have even more appreciation for the young people of that era, who were to become "The Greatest Generation."

Little would they know that within one and one-half years of their high school graduation, their world would be turned upside down by a World War. Never would their lives be the same again. I found it interesting to see these young people (my parents and their peers) possessing and expressing the same hopes, quirks, dreams, mischiefs, desires, and optimism that all eighteen-year-olds just naturally hold. I reflect on that time in my own life, and it seems so long ago. But I regress.

So, my mom moved to Odessa with her family from East Texas the summer of 1938, just before her sophomore year in high school. She was the new girl in town, and by all accounts, quite "the looker." I remember my dad telling me about the day he returned to Odessa from working all summer up on the farm near Byers, Texas — when a good buddy sought him out and told him, "Charlie, you gotta meet this new girl, Minnie Fay. Her family just moved into town. And, man, is she pretty!" So, within a couple of days, they did meet (the class size was around one hundred, and both were in the band); and from what I gather, they must have dated on and off some that first year — their sophomore year. From entries in her yearbook, I see she evidently did not want to be tied down to one particular fellow at the time. Lots of boys were potential suitors but one thing was very clear — she was equally liked by both the guys and girls in her class.

My mom was sweet, innocent, naïve, caring, fun ... and *bowlegged!* She must have embraced "her condition" (because it was mentioned in several yearbook entries), and that probably just added to her charm. Another thing I noticed in the yearbook signings was the

Charlie Jr. and Minnie Fay (circa 1940)

genuineness, kindness, and frankness of the entries written to her. One guy actually wrote, "To a swell gal with a swell figure ... " Oh boy! Another fellow signed, "The best of luck. Here's hoping for a kiss before the year is over." Several times my mom was referred to as "Hot Cha" — a slang term of the day which meant "flashy, vivacious, attractive." It was evident my mom was also one of the good girls, and "hands-off" with the boys, which must have made her all the more alluring. By the end of her first year at Odessa High School, she was voted Junior Class Secretary.

Now my father was also pretty popular and was lead actor in the school's one act plays, both as a junior and senior. He tried to persuade my mom to try out for the play their senior year by signing in her junior yearbook, "We sure could have a lot of fun together." She did *not* try out, and I surmise that going out with the footballers and her girlfriends had more appeal. But I do know my mom and dad still did "court" a bit their senior year. And even though my dad was voted Class Favorite, my mom still enjoyed playing the field. Another entry my dad wrote in her yearbook was above her class picture: "Minnie — *'Cold Cha'*." Hmm…

So, as the story is told, graduation came, and it was time for the annual senior class trip. Busloads of new graduates headed off on a weeklong trip to Washington, DC, to see the Capitol, the White House, and other historical sites of the area. Quite an adventure for these young Odessans, many of whom I'm sure had never been outside the state of Texas. My dad got to go, but for some reason my mom did not make the trip. While up there though, my dad, with what little spending money he had, purchased several little gifts (necklace, bracelet, DC mementos, etc.) specifically with my mom in mind. So, the day they all got back, my dad arranged a date with her to "go out for a coke" and tell her all about the trip and give her these little gifts. He got permission to borrow the family Model T from his dad, put the collection of little presents in the glove compartment, and headed off to pick up Minnie Fay for the fun evening that was sure to be had. They did the Coke thing, and then my dad took her to West County Park so they could "park" and visit. Then, as my dad told me, they were enjoying catching up, when he asked her if he could kiss her. My mom said, "I don't think so." He just sat there. "What? Really?! I've got some things I want to give you." My mom said, "No. I'd rather not." So, without saying another word, my disappointed and frustrated dad started up the car and began driving. My mom asked, "Where are we going?" Looking straight ahead, he said, "I'm taking your sweet little patootie home, sister!" And he did.

P.S. Within six months, my mom transferred college from Sul Ross State to Texas Tech to follow my dad there. One year later they were married. My dad told me many years later that my mother never did get those gifts, as he thoroughly enjoyed flattering other little ladies in town who greatly appreciated the gesture.

Mom and Dad – Hawaii 1975

# *10*

# VICTOR IN NAME — VICTOR IN LIFE

In the fall of 1965, I was a fifteen-year-old whippersnapper, first year in high school ... just got my driver's license, spreading my wings a little bit, and my biggest cares were trying to figure out how "geometry" works and who to invite to Odessa High's Homecoming Dance. Some 8,500 miles to the west, twenty-nine-year-old US Marine fighter pilot Victor Barris was flying his supersonic fixed-wing 4F Phantom jet into enemy territory on his first combat tour in Vietnam ... dropping bombs, rockets, and napalm in support of American and South Vietnamese ground troops fighting enemy soldiers from North Vietnam and The Viet Cong.

Three years later, I was at Texas Tech University relishing my freshman year of college (big-time college sports, dorm life, coeds/new friends, intra-mural football, and organizations to join) and feeling pretty smug about life. I had a college deferment from any military service requirement for at least four years and was experiencing the carefree life and independence away from home for the first time. In the meantime, Fighter Squadron Leader Barris was on his second combat tour of duty in Vietnam battling the North Vietnamese Army and defending freedom and the American way of life that I took for granted.

In March, 1974, I was in Hawaii working in advertising for the Honolulu Star Bulletin-Advertiser newspapers — my first job right out of college. On weekends I'd go snorkeling at Hanauma Bay or hiking in the mountains of Manoa Valley … then to church on Sundays. Some 6,000 miles away, "Deacon" (his call sign because he was a church-goer) Barris was in the midst of his third and final combat tour of Vietnam, flying his supersonic jets off the USS Midway Aircraft Carrier on reconnaissance missions, and navigating his way up and down the coasts of North and South Vietnam. He was also "on standby for other duties" that might necessitate immediate action, should they arise.

By the time his tours of duty in Vietnam were over, he'd flown some 500 missions and had been able to walk away from them all. But US Marine Major Victor Barris could not walk away from the memories seared into his soul… memories and images that will never go away. Yet, Providence still had plans for this good man of faith.

One summer evening (2023) I had the great privilege of meeting and talking with this spry eighty-seven-year-old distinguished war veteran. Victor is the father

Victor Barris with his F4 Phantom jet

of the wife of my church pastor in Cleburne, Texas. So that was our connection. I write short stories, his storied life is full of them, and he agreed to share some of them with me. Before we really got started, I shared with Victor a few things about myself — that I'm a strong patriot, I love our country dearly, I love the Lord who saved me, I *very much* appreciated his service in the military, and I felt very honored to talk with him. I explained to him I would have joined the military if drafted; but by the time I got out of college, the Armed Forces had gone to an all-volunteer system of recruitment. I told him to feel free to share (or not to share) anything on his heart and mind as I probed. Victor was easy going, quite conversant, had a great memory, and extremely humbled by my desire to tell some of the tales of his extraordinary life. Because we both are committed to Jesus Christ as our Lord and Savior, we connected easily and smoothly.

Ever since Victor was a little kid growing up in east Los Angeles, he wanted to be a fighter pilot and fly fast jets. Upon high school graduation, he took two years of schooling at a local community college and then enlisted in the Navy for pilot training (a four-year commitment). Victor was one sharp cookie and passed his training schools with flying colors. Over his twenty-year career in the Armed Forces, he was stationed various places for schooling, instructing, and service (Naval Air Station, Pensacola, Florida; Marine Corps Air Station, Cherry Point, North Carolina; twice at Chase Field, Beeville, Texas; and later at Camp Pendleton, San Diego, California) … and, of course, he had his tours of duty in Vietnam. It was at his first stop in Beeville that he met the former Joanne Baker on a blind date. She was attending Baylor University (Waco) at the time, but they clicked, stayed in touch, married in 1962, had four kids, and have been together now for some sixty-one years … and they still like each other!

Flying out of Da Nang Air Base – Vietnam War

He loved flying those state-of-the-art F4 Phantom jets while serving his country and defending democracy. It was his duty and calling. The F4 Phantoms were like the "Cadillac" of all fighter planes — with a top speed of over 2,000 m.p.h. and 35,000 pounds of thrust. These planes were so fast and powerful they could easily break the sound barrier and outrace the bullets shot at them from behind. As alluded to earlier, on his first tour of duty in Vietnam, starting in 1965, his job was to fly low (500 feet and below) and fast (1,000+ mph) to provide ground support to the American/South Vietnamese troops in the midst of combat. His payload would vary somewhat depending on the mission but could include five-inch diameter Zuni rockets, 250-pound bombs (some leftover from WWII), AIM-9 Sidewinder missiles, and oft times incendiary napalm (a volatile, viscous gel used to decimate and burn up anything in its path).

One time he almost shot *himself* down. Seems as if when he was making this particular bombing run, flying fast and really low, he released the bombs, and one of them malfunctioned — the expanding fin at one end of the bomb that was supposed open up and slow its descent did *not* open up. So, the bomb flew as fast as the plane was going and descending straight forward into the ground, exploding on impact and blowing debris and shrapnel right up into the underside of Vic's plane. He could tell something was wrong. He had fellow Phantoms fly below him and look to see if they saw anything unusual. They said, "Yeah … looks like you have a fairly large hole exposed underneath, but can't tell much more." On the ground and upon inspection, they found remnants of the bomb itself and knew what had happened.

On another particular sortie, Barris encountered so much gunfire and flak it seemed as if he was being peppered by enemy bullets at will. He felt the plane shuddering and making noises he knew "did not sound right." He barely made it back to base at Da Nang. He'd been shot at, shot up, and by the grace of God, *not* shot down. Upon landing and inspection, he counted 147 bullet holes in his plane before losing count. Then the maintenance crew "just hauled the plane off for junk."

At the time, Victor felt he was just doing his job as any loyal Marine soldier should do. Most times he was able to remove himself from the moment, release his payload, then fly on to his next target or base … believ-

Major Barris (R) with his "GIBS"

ing all along he was helping fellow Americans survive and accomplish their goal of destroying the enemy on the ground as he was from the air. Frequently, he and his navigator (GIBS — Guy In Back-Seat) would see reports of how "successful" their mission had been. That was determined by American soldiers physically walking among the dead bodies for a headcount and recording the number of enemy soldiers killed by the raid. The term used? *KBMA Killed by Marine Air.* Over time, Victor began to have disturbing, mixed emotions whenever he would see those reports. But it was easy to justify his way of thinking: *He knew he had a job to do. That's what he signed up for. It's either kill or be killed. He was fighting for his family and country and democracy and freedom for all peoples. He was helping fellow Americans on the battlefield who needed his help in stopping the godless Communists from taking over Vietnam, then the world.* Then in other solemn, reflective, conflicted moments *these* thoughts would come: *Is not every life precious to God? Does not our Maker know every one of us, even from our mothers' womb? Jesus loves ALL the little children of the world, right? Did not Jesus die for all peoples no matter… Love your enemies … For God so loved the world…*

Victor was also struggling in his own spiritual life. A believer from early in life, and with all that was going on around him, he felt unsettled; and this uneasiness in his spirit kept growing. He even wondered, "Is this what God in heaven wants me to continue doing?" Though doubts were creeping into his thinking about his missions (and purpose in life), Victor continued on doing his job and was very successful in what he did. Then, a *break did come* when he was given the opportunity work in the area of "Reconnaissance/Photo Combat." No more shooting rockets or dropping bombs or napalm, but using infrared photography and night-time sorties to pinpoint enemy targets and positions for the bombers to follow. Though it, too, was extremely hazardous, this was a good change for him and rested better in his restlessness. Later, Victor was promoted to the rank of Major and became the officer in charge of a

squadron on the USS Midway Aircraft Carrier. He was awarded the annual Decoration of Excellent Achievement of Marine Corps Aviation citation for his skill, courage, leadership, and devotion to God and country.

Though he can't remember *exactly* when, it was during this time that Victor came across an iconic picture in a magazine that shook him to his very being. It was the Pulitzer Prize winning photograph titled "The Terror of War" ("Napalm Girl") — taken in June, 1972, in Trang Bang, Vietnam, of a nine-year-old Vietnamese girl running naked and screaming away from her village that had just been bombed by napalm. In the background one could see the huge inferno engulfing the small village, bringing death and destruction to innocent Vietnamese villagers. That photograph was a turning point for many a soul, including Victor's ... maybe even a watershed moment for the sentiments of millions of Americans back home and countless millions around the world. The piercing visual image of that innocent child desperately fleeing from incineration penetrated Vic's heart like nothing else ever before. Devilish thoughts started racing through Vic's mind: *"Could that have come from one of my earlier raids? I was there, maybe, I think. I don't want to know. I can't know ... Oh dear God ... surely not. Please not me."* The thoughts never went away.

As commanding officer of his squadron, and a man of faith, he felt responsible for all the men on his ship. On occasion, he even filled in for the ship's chaplain a few times in his absence. In 1975, Victor lost a pilot in a Recon mission from his warship, and it really hit him hard. As the commanding officer, Victor ended up giving this fallen soldier's eulogy on board. Though he felt he could have done a better job in his oration, he was complimented in his presentation to the point of others even suggesting when he retires from the military someday maybe he ought to think about going into the ministry somewhere. Although he self-effacingly dismissed the idea, it did get him to thinking... well, who knows? God knew.

So, when the day came to move on from his decorated military career after twenty years of service in 1976, he and Joanne moved back home to Beeville, Texas. Ol' Deacon Victor got involved with their church and soon was asked to head up the "Building Committee" for a new Activity Center. So that's what he did, and he was good at it, too. The gym was built, and Victor oversaw the various activities in the facility — whether it be roller skating and games for the kids, or churchwide socials for congregants. Once again, he'd proven himself to be a leader who gets things done. Soon church leaders invited Victor to become even more involved by joining their staff and becoming their Minister of Education. He accepted, and shortly thereafter, he was off to school in Nashville for some "formal training" in church work. He had found his new calling. Within three years, Sunday School attendance at First Baptist Church, Beeville, had grown from some 200 attendees to over 500. And it was all well with his soul.

During my three hours of conversation with Victor Barris, the only time I could tell he became emotional (and actually teared up ... and me along with him) was when he brought up the Napalm girl. I personally remember the haunting image myself from the magazines/newspapers of some fifty years ago. How can one forget that? It's still there for Victor.

The girl in the picture, Phan Thi Kim Phuc, did survive. She faced numerous surgeries, hospital stays, and years of recovery; and most days Kim still battles severe pain as a result of her burns and injuries. But in 1982, things changed for Kim. She found a New Testament in a library somewhere that led her to become a true Christian and embrace the power of forgiveness. Eventually she studied medicine, moved to Cuba, and trained as a pharmacist. In Havana she met another Vietnamese student Bu Huy Toan, and they became engaged. The couple married in 1992, and successfully sought political asylum in Canada. In 1997, she established the first Kim Phuc Foundation in the United States, with the aim of providing medical and psychological assistance to child victims of war.

Kim is now a UNESCO Goodwill Ambassador and founder of The KIM Foundation International based in Ontario, Canada. In 2008 Kim Phuc told National Public Radio: "*Forgiveness made me free from hatred. I still have many scars on my body and severe pain most days but my heart is cleansed. Napalm is very powerful, but faith, forgiveness, and love are much more powerful. We would not have war at all if everyone could learn how to live with true love, hope and forgiveness. If that little girl in the picture can do it, ask yourself: Can you?*"

How could Kim do this? Only by the grace of God. How did Major Victor Barris survive 500 fighter jet missions without being shot down? Only by the grace of God. The Maker of heaven and earth had other plans, much grander plans for that nine-year-old innocent victim of war. He had much bigger plans for Phantom Jet Fighter pilot Victor Barris too … plans for good and not for evil, to give them both a future and a hope … plans with eternal value and purpose.

*Genesis 50:20 says it the purest and truest in that what was meant for evil, God meant it for good. That's the God they serve … and the One who orchestrated their stories from the very beginning.*

# 11

# DON'T WANT TO MEAT AGAIN

I'm not exactly sure where it all started, but I have an idea — this growing aversion to meat. It was possibly when I was about ten-years-old and with my mom, when she was visiting a neighbor friend in Odessa. This lady friend had a platter of goodies in full display, ready for the taking and eating — various cheeses, crackers, fruits, deli-type meats. I saw one sliced symmetrical item that looked a little different, so I thought I'd give it a try. Very unusual texture and taste. Hmm. "Mom, what's this?" She hem-hawed around, but finally in subdued manner, answered, "Tongue. It's cow's tongue." Oh, my goodness, I almost lost it right then … I learned something through this though — always ask before you taste.

A couple years later Mom and I took a trip up to Mount Rushmore and the Badlands National Park in South Dakota. While there we took in the park restaurant overlooking the range below, scattered with bison, prong-horns, and other indigenous animals. The restaurant's specialty: "Buffalo Burgers." Now I liked a good ol' fashioned hamburger alright (so long as I didn't know/think about how the meat got in there), but *Buffalo* – I don't think so. At age eleven or twelve, I'm starting to get it. I didn't get their specialty. I opted for the grilled cheese sandwich just fine, thank you.

When I was in college, during summer break in 1970, my buddy Gordon and I ventured to Europe for about six weeks. We traveled all over, and to one special place about an hour northeast of Paris. His mom's family was from this little French village, and so we got to meet his aunts, uncles, and cousins for the first time. They all only spoke French. Now, with Gordon not knowing any French (he'd taken some German in college), and my having had a couple of semesters of French, it fell to me to try my meager hand at conversing. With that good ol' West Texas accent of mine, my "parlez-vouses" were probably interpreted "what say you?" more often than not. Anyway, they treated us to a hearty family-style meal at their house in the country. The brown gravy-covered entree definitely had a distinct pungent taste to it. I'm thinking I'm not sure I've ever tasted this before. I better slow down. I asked our hosts in my broken Francais what kind of meat we were enjoying. With proud satisfaction, Gordon's uncle proclaimed "C'est cheval. Tres bien, non?" "Cheval!?" "Oui, Monsieur." I almost gagged... we were eating *HORSE*! I tried to be as inconspicuous as I could shifting my sliver of horsey under my bread and into my napkin. I watched as Gordon emptied his plate with one piece of meat left. Savoring this last piece of a free home-cooked meal, he put the bite in his mouth, and as he began chewing, I said to Gordon, "Well, buddy, guess what you've just-a-been eatin'? Giddy up, partner... it's horse!" That piece of equine shot out of Gordon's mouth like a spitball out of a peashooter. It reminds me of the scene in the movie "Funny Farm" wherein Chevy Chase had just set the record for eating the most "lamb fries" at one sitting ... and then finding out what those little morsels were. Look it up.

A number of years later, I was invited for dinner over to friend's house in Nashville. Now, I knew Steve was an avid hunter, but I was unsuspecting of anything out of the ordinary, when asked if I liked chili okay. Not my favorite, but loaded up with ketchup, onions, and cheese, I'm good. Real good, actually. So, about the second spoonful of *this* homemade chili ...

do I mention the distinct taste of the meat we're having? Steve asks, "You ever had venison before? Well, you have now. Yeah, it's real fresh, too. Killed and cleaned that deer myself just this week." I about lost it again. As they say, timing is everything, and it did not help that only recently I had

"Bowl of Bambi?" Think I'll pass.

accompanied a couple of friends' kids one afternoon to see the big screen re-release of "Bambi." I had too much pride to tell my hosts it was *me* who was crying during the shooting scene … with those kids consoling me! Time to man up, Charlie boy!

Back around 1975 when I was living and working in Hawaii, I had lobster for the first time (too expensive for my taste and bank account). It was steak and lobster night out at this gala I was invited to in Honolulu. I have to say, the white, fully-steamed lobster tail with garlic herb drawn butter was delicious. So, I thought I'd do that again, maybe, on a very special occasion. That time came in 1978 when my mom and I went out for dinner with some special friends in Washington, DC. They picked out this upscale seafood restaurant and insisted on us getting *anything* on the menu — their treat, no matter the cost. Well, I perused the menu and their specialty was fresh broiled Maine lobster with French-inspired sage and tarragon cream sauce. Well, why not! Fifteen minutes later, here came my lobster — the *whole* lobster placed right in front of me. I was speechless. I was expecting only the white meat of the tail, like I'd had before. Well, I looked down again at my lobster, and I'm telling you, his beady eyes were looking right back at me as if to say, "You don't want to do this, do you?" I tried to figure out how I was going to handle this with my friends, when I glanced down again, and I thought I saw a couple of this lobster's antennae moving around. I about lost it again ("Waiter, could I get a grilled cheese, please?"). My friends sensed my dilemma and had the waiter take my lobster out of sight and de-tail it for me. I was pretty okay after that. It was still a beautiful evening with my friends, but that was the last time I ever ordered lobster.

Finally, a couple years ago, my Black friend Tony invited me and wife Carolyn to join him and his wife Tabitha for some *soul food* after church at this homey, cafeteria-style restaurant in south Fort Worth. His treat. Okay! Sounds fun! Well, we went in, and we were definitely out of our comfort zone. Out of the hundred or so folks there, we were the only two Whites. But the people could not have been more hospitable. I got fried catfish, mashed potatoes, green beans, cole slaw, and all the fixins, and it was delicious. Not Tony. He just had to order chitlins, neck bone, and oxtail soup … and, then, of course, he *would* sit right across the table from me. I had a hard time enjoying my fried catfish seeing an oxtail hanging (or was it wagging?) over the side of Tony's too-small bowl. But still very glad we went. Learned things. A couple months later, it was our treat to the same place with one condition: "Tony, no 'wild, exotic' stuff, okay?" He agreed. He easily made a meal out of fried chicken and meat loaf, stewed tomatoes/okra, collard greens, and cornbread. He was quite okay with that, and we all had a great meal together.

I confess I'm all mixed up and missing out on some good eatin' I know not of. However, all things considered, I could easily be a vegetarian. That being said, I do have an occasional hankerin' for a good ol' fashioned hamburger from Hef's Hamburgers in Sweetwater, Texas, or a puffy, crispy beef taco from El Fenix Mexican Restaurant in Burleson, Texas, or a pulled pork sandwich from Top Choice BBQ in Greeneville, Tennessee. One thing for sure, though, you'll never catch me eating *anything that slithers or dangles*.

## *12*

# TOO LATE IN
# SAYING GOODBYE

N ow that I'm seventy-three, it's really starting to hit home a little closer —
this feeling that each day we are given is a blessing. Especially when I
hear of a former classmate or a long-ago friend passing away. So, lately I've
been reaching out to people from my past to reconnect and to let them know
of a pleasant memory or positive influence or fun anecdote I have of them.
Anyway, I got to thinking of people that are gone now, and if somehow our
paths had crossed earlier, there would be certain things I'd loved to have
shared with them before it was too late.

Gentle Giant Craig

For instance, and this goes back some forty-
eight years (1975), there was a guy named Craig
I'd known since my days at Crockett Jr. High in
Odessa. There I was, safe and secure in Hawaii,
reading the newspaper I worked for (Honolulu Star
Bulletin-Advertiser), when I came across a short
article and headline about an oilfield explosion in
Goldsmith, Texas, killing a twenty-five-year-old oil-
field worker named Craig Fife. What!? Not Craig!
He was *BIG* and strong and such a good guy. I

mean, he was probably the biggest guy I knew growing up (maybe around six-feet six-inches and 250 pounds). For a wiry little fellow like myself, that's big. But Craig was a gentle giant. And though I didn't play football, I always appreciated the way he treated me as his equal and friend, even though I was not on his level of athleticism. I would have liked to have told him just that. Should have, but never got around to it.

Then there was Jan. I liked her in the seventh grade ... a lot. Really pretty, long black hair, and a cheerleader. Sweet gal. I just seemed to play better for my basketball team (the Fightin' Red and White Crockett Colts), when I knew she was cheering for and watching me. I was too shy to ask her for a phone number to call her up sometime. But I was gonna tell her so (with trusty wife Carolyn at my side) at our high school's fiftieth reunion. Then I found out Jan had passed away a few months beforehand. Sadly, I never had that chance, and I deeply regret that.

Favorite Cheerleader Jan

I knew Terry from Austin Elementary. He was my nemesis/friend. Anything I did, he wanted to do. He was pretty much my equal athletically, and we competed a bit for the attention of the little ladies. In the fifth grade, he once purposely jammed a pencil in my kneecap (was he jealous of my month-long relationship with Katrina?). I still have a remnant piece of pencil lead in my left knee to prove it. The thing is, I did not know of his horrific family life and how *good* I had it. Let's just say, whereas I had love, encouragement, and hugs from my mom and dad, Terry had just

Friendly Rival Terry

the opposite. His mother died early in his life, and he lived with his grandmother and two brothers. Yeah, he had a father alright — one who was extremely abusive to him and his brothers, both verbally and physically. No wonder he sought refuge at the home of classmates whenever he could. Terry's next older brother committed suicide in high school. What does that tell you? I had no idea. I was totally ignorant of his home life, and I'm so sorry for not being kinder, gentler, and a better friend to this struggling soul.

Fun and Spunky
Lou Ann

The first girl to ever write me a "Love Note" was Lou Ann when we were both in the fifth grade ... wanted to hold my hand, she did. I was flattered by the attention she gave me, and I think we met for a picture show together a time or two at the Ector Theater downtown. Around 2005, I ran into her mom in Odessa when visiting my dad and found out that Lou Ann lived in Comanche, Texas, and worked as a nurse there at the local hospital. My daughter played percussion in the Glen Rose High School band, and it so happened that Glen Rose was scheduled to play Comanche in football that October. I knew we'd be going to the game. Lou Ann's mom gave me her number, and I called her up to see if she might could meet us at the game, or better yet join us for dinner. She said she'd love to and would try, but her hours at the hospital varied and she'd have to let us know. Well, try as hard as she may, she had to work and couldn't get free. "Next time, then. Real soon. Okay!" I wanted her to meet my wife and let her know I always liked her. She was a fun friend I admired, and I never forgot her spunk! The next month I was working a flight with a new crewmember on one of my trips. When I asked where she lived, she told me she was from Comanche. I said "Oh, wow. I know one person from Comanche. Just got reconnected with her after decades. Do you happen to know my friend Lou Ann ... a nurse at the hospital there?"

My co-worker's face just flushed. She said, "I don't know how to tell you this, but, yes, I knew Lou Ann. She died of a heart attack last week. I'm so sorry." I was stunned. I mean, I had *just talked with her* on the phone a couple weeks earlier for the first time in forty-five years... and it hit me again — this feeling. Lou Ann was the only person I knew growing up that was born the same month as me (July, 1950). Once again, I endeavored to count my blessings every day.

Then there was Paul. Not really my friend or non-friend, just a classmate in various classes here and there from elementary on up through high school. We just ran in different circles. But Paul died a couple years ago; and if I had had the chance to say something to him, this would be it: "Paul, though we were more 'acquaintances' than friends per se, there are two things I always admired about you. One is, remember in the fifth or sixth grade when you tried out for our elementary school basketball team? Coach Harrison picked the top ten

One Determined Paul

players out of the twenty or so kids trying out to be on the team. I was picked and you were not. Coach Harrison then addressed you and the others as such: 'Now boys, you did NOT make this team. I encourage you to work at it and to try out again next year. However, if you want to stick around and practice (limited) with us, you can... but you most likely will NOT ever even get in a game — the whole year! You will sit on the bench the entire time.' Well, you, Paul, were the only boy who stayed. And I remember, you got to play in one game for a couple of minutes... toward the end of one of our last games when the outcome had already been decided. You looked lost and did not play very well, but you never gave up. Good for you!"

Paul was also one sharp guy and one of the first kids I'd ever known who knew early on what he wanted be when he grew up. We were in the seventh grade and both got braces on our teeth from the same dentist/orthodontist, a Dr. Crane. Paul told me that's what he was gonna be someday — a dentist. I was envious that he knew as a twelve-year-old what he wanted to be. And he did become that. He had a successful dental practice in Odessa for some four decades. Not me. At age twenty-six I became a Flight Attendant for an airline for thirty-four years. To each his own. I regret not stopping by his dental office on 8th Street when in Odessa to tell him those fond remembrances I have of a guy I only knew from afar. Could have, should have.

True Friend Marilee

Finally, there was sweet Marilee, another classmate I had in various classes all the way through school. She was smart, kind, dependable, and personable — just a really good friend to anyone who knew her. She was the kind of really good friend who might even tell you the truth about something you'd rather not hear. Right? Well, that was Marilee to me in the seventh grade. I guess I was a pretty popular guy alright… at least, I thought so. My first year at Crockett Jr. High, I was selected Class Favorite Runner-Up. I even had my picture taken with Vicki (she was the girl Runner-Up Favorite) for the school memory book. Vicki was so pretty, and I was so intimidated. We hardly spoke. Anyway, I got to thinking and believing just how "popular" I was, and it showed. I became a little too cocky, a little too arrogant and smug in my misguided self-importance. I did not realize this. You know what my true friend Marilee did? She came up to me one day in the hall at school and said, "You know what you are, Charlie? You are conceited and you're a little too big for your britches, good friend." I didn't even know what the word *conceited* meant. But I sensed it was not good. I went home, looked it up in the dictionary, and was humbled big-time. Actually, I was a little embarrassed and ashamed. Yeah, I could see it. Not good. I *DO NOT WANT* to be that way! From that point on, and this was in 1962, after Marilee's comment to me, I decided I was gonna change my ways. I definitely had my work cut out for me. Eighth grade … I was not selected anything. But by ninth grade, when I had tried focusing more on others instead of my selfish self, and tried being kinder and more genuinely friendly to all classmates no matter, I got selected Most Dependable Boy for our class. I liked me better then, too. I'd never told Marilee, I don't think, even at school reunions, what a positive influence she had been to me.

So, in the summer of 2020, I was talking with a mutual friend on the phone, and Marilee's name came up. My friend told me she thought she could get Marilee's number. She did, and I called Marilee and left a voicemail message to call me back, if she would like, when convenient. A couple days later, I got a sweet text message from Marilee saying that would be great, let's do visit, but that she had a sore throat that just came on, was hoarse, and couldn't talk right then. She said she would call me in few days when she got her voice back… much looking forward to catching up. I never heard back. I waited a few days more and never heard back. I called her again, maybe ten days later. Her phone went straight to voicemail. Then that sad night in June 2020, wife Carolyn asks me if I had known a classmate named Marilee (Class 1968) from Odessa High? What!? "Yeah, just saw on Facebook that she died yesterday from COVID." "Oh No! — I had just been in text communication with her last week! We were gonna talk!" I didn't even know what to say. I was so taken aback. It took me a few days to recover and process my thoughts … that feeling returned once again. Then I recalled reading what Eleanor Roosevelt once famously said so long ago (and I've written in a previous article), that still stands true now: *Yesterday Is History, Tomorrow Is a Mystery, Today Is a Gift. That's Why It's Called "The Present."*

So, I endeavor to not let these times go by when there's opportunity to say a kind, uplifting word of a fond memory or encouragement to others we know in this journey we call life.

## 13

# YOU DON'T KNOW WHERE THE WIND BLOWS

Anumber of years ago, my wife Carolyn and I lived in a rural setting and savored the quiet, slower pace of life in the country. The occasional deer dashing across our caliche driveway, the varied songbirds filling the air with their unique trills, and the wondrous sight of countless stars illuminating the dark nighttime sky — it's these things and much more that lured us to the country life.

Getting along with neighbors, on the other hand, can, on occasion, be a challenge and a little tricky. And those relationships can change from time to time as well. So, it was with us a number of years ago, when something came up concerning our property and one of our neighbor's adjoining properties. Decades earlier, we had bought two of the three adjacent parcels of land (approximately 15 acres apiece), and "Wayne" bought the other fifteen-acre plot adjoining ours. Same owner/seller. We built our houses far enough away from each other that we hardly ever saw or heard each other's goings-on and had complete privacy. We got along pretty good, would talk every once in a while, and knew each other's phone number in case of emergency.

When we purchased this land from the original owner, deed restrictions were put in place by the lawyer who drew up the purchasing contract and the owner/seller. These restrictions were for the purpose of protecting the way of country living and the rural way of life. In essence, the seller (who lived nearby) wanted no commercial activity taking place in the area — no used car lots, hog farms, restaurants, mobile home parks, or body repair shops. We agreed, as we wanted to keep it that way ourselves, and all signed the contract accordingly.

So, one not-so-good day a few years later, we were shocked to find out that Wayne and his wife were in the midst of building a so-called "Event Venue/Wedding Barn" on their property — approximately thirty feet or so from our adjoining common border. They did not tell us of this, as my wife found out when she ran into another nearby neighbor while shopping in town. Carolyn was caught off guard when she was asked, "What do you think about the new 'Wedding Barn' that Wayne and his wife are building on their land?" What! What is this now?!

When Carolyn got home and told me the news, we got in our car and drove down the road past our neighbor's property, and there it was — the tall, erect wooden framework of a large structure some thirty to forty feet high. It was obvious this place was being built for celebratory events such as weddings, graduation parties, family reunions … and all the things that would naturally accompany such a venue: loud music/noise, partying, drinking, bright lights, traffic, debris, revelry, what have you. Exactly why we moved to the country — *to get away from such things!* As we viewed the partially completed construction of the building, we both had this sickening feeling in the pit of our stomachs.

If this project were to happen, our lifestyle and surrounding neighbors' lifestyle could be significantly altered; and from our perspective, definitely not for the good. And it very well could *lower* the property value of our life's biggest investment. As any long-time neighbor should do (when such a project would affect the neighborhood), we'd think the proper thing to do would be to let one's neighbors know of your *plans. Why did not we not know of any of this?* Others did.

I *think* I know … because he wanted to get the thing built one way or another, and then what could we do? I think he also figured there would probably be some resistance, especially from us (his closest neighbors) and others, and he didn't want to hear it. We were at a loss on knowing what our next step should be, except we knew before long we needed to confront Wayne. Then Carolyn recalled, "Weren't there some kind of deed restrictions we all signed that very well might apply here?" *Yes indeed! That's it!* It'd been years since we'd even thought about that. I retrieved our copy of the agreement I had in safe keeping in the house. I read through the contract (with deed restrictions), and in what little I understood of legal-type things, I thought this *does* apply. I believe Wayne and his wife are in violation of the contract by constructing the building. Oh my … this is going to be quite the confrontation.

I did have a couple of real estate/lawyer-types look over the contract, and they both gave the same opinion: Yes, they felt we did have the legal right to challenge their project and were in right standing. I also tried to put myself in Wayne's (and wife's) shoes, and maybe this was their way of thinking: "Here we are, way out in the country, we're about to retire from our regular jobs, and a dream we've had for a while now has been to construct a building/venue to host parties, weddings, reunions. This could be a lot of fun, putting this on, and making money to help supplement our retirement. We have friends who've done this. We know how this works. We have the land/space … so why not? It's nobody's business but ours." I did understand that. But, I say, *it became our business, too*, when the venture could very much affect the ambience of the countryside and our neighborhood.

So, a few days later, and after a couple more consultations with people in the know and prayer with my Sunday School Class for me to do and say the right thing, a supportive neighbor, "John" (as a witness and moral support), picked me up in his pickup and we went over to see Wayne unannounced. Dogs barked, but no one came to the door. My neighbor drove me back home, but a few minutes later the phone rang. It was Wayne asking what I wanted (he must have seen us) and why I came over. It was obvious he did not want to talk with me in person. But I persisted. So, John and I went *back* over there within twenty minutes of that first attempt. He was less than cordial to me when I asked him about his plans for the structure he was building. "It's an 'Event Venue.' What's that to you?" I tried to explain I had concerns about his plans and asked him why he did not let us know of this. He said it was none of my business and he could do whatever he wanted on his own property. I then suggested he look up the deed restrictions attached to the contract we all signed when we purchased our properties years earlier, and that I felt it very much applied to what he was doing. He came at me again with, "What do you want me to do! Tear down the *damn* building!?" I replied, "What I *am saying* is that you need to read the contract, and I think you will see there are issues with your plans." I also told him in strong, no uncertain terms "*I will protect my property and my investment … whatever it takes.*" I did not threaten him, but he knew where I was coming from.

I think possibly he was embarrassed that we knew he was going behind our backs, and that he did not recall the deed restrictions. After this fifteen-minute uneasy confrontation, he basically ushered me and my companion out the door … telling *me* I was no longer welcome in his house. It was such an emotional, vitriolic encounter, I was completely enervated and could hardly talk as we made the short drive back to my house. It was probably around 5:00 p.m. by this time. I felt very sad and anxious because of the big mess this was becoming … with hurt feelings of all involved. I also felt a little sorry for Wayne and his wife because I knew we had become an obstacle to their dreams. But this whole thing would never have come about if he'd been upfront with me from the beginning. I began to think, well, I guess the next step will probably involve getting a lawyer, and that could be expensive. Ugh …

Shortly thereafter, Carolyn returned home after running some errands and asked me how it went as she'd been praying for me the whole time. I told her it didn't go so well — in fact, it was an acrimonious, gut-wrenching fifteen minutes. And I'm not sure where we go from here except: "We gotta pray. Big-time." I know the Lord we serve is bigger than any problem or dilemma we're facing, but this was very tough and in the moment. So, we decided to go out on our front porch swing, hold hands, and fervently, earnestly ask God for His intervention somehow in this tangled situation. Too big for us, but not too big for Him. We cried out to the Lord in submission and contriteness, because our hearts and words were not meant to cause conflict. We wanted to be good neighbors to Wayne and his wife. We prayed to the Lord Jesus saying we knew that *everything* we have — our house, our land, our cars, our good health, our relationships, our lives … all of it, is really His anyway. Asking our Father in Heaven for His dealing with this situation and our dilemma, however He would choose, and that His will to be done … Amen. We just gave it all to Him.

Then we just sat there in our porch swing quietly for a few minutes contemplating the hard events of the day and wondering what comes next. About that time the amazing, omniscient God we serve was orchestrating things we could not have known. The winds started picking up a little bit … looking like a storm might be brewing. Soon there were small, swirling gusts of wind that seemed to pick up in intensity as we sat there anticipating a possible thunderstorm coming our way. With partial sunlight peeking through the clouds in the midst, there came a couple of stronger rain-filled whirlwinds moving quickly past our front yard area. Like a mighty wind, another sudden gust came blowing through. It was then, in the distance, we saw a bright flash and heard a piercing, crackling sound, followed by a loud thud. My thought was it must have been lightning striking a tree or something of the sort. We hurried from the porch seeking refuge from the storm into the house.

About ten minutes later, my phone rang. It was Wayne. His words to me were: "You won't have to worry about the Wedding Barn anymore. The wind blew it completely down, and we won't be rebuilding." The only words I remember saying, before we were disconnected, were "I'm sorry for your loss." What had God wrought? It was hard to believe what had just happened. I felt so unworthy, humbled, undeserving of such an awesome display of God's omnipotence and divine intervention on our behalf. It's then He seemed to say to me: "Son, this is not about you. Remember you are a child of the King, and I know all about these things and move in mys-

T-shirt I was wearing throughout that fateful day

terious ways. You are to tell others about my love for them, and that I work all things together for good for those that love me. Trust in Me, and rest in My peace." I had just experienced the gentle, yet all-powerful Hand of God upon my life ... and in awesome gratitude, I sat down and wept.

*"You don't know where the wind blows ... In the same way,*
*you don't know what God will do – and He makes everything happen."*
*Ecclesiastes 11:15 (ERV)*

## *14*

# THAT WAS A
# SHOCKER ALRIGHT!

In the spring of 1994, wife Carolyn and I knew we'd be moving to the Glen Rose, Texas, area with our two young kids in June of that year. We were living in Middle Tennessee at the time and visiting her parents in Crossville, Tennessee, a couple hours' drive away. As we were enjoying our visit with the family, the TV was set on the Trinity Broadcasting Network channel on low volume, when all of a sudden there was this scholarly, middle-aged gentleman with a smooth, strong voice discussing this "Creation Museum" near Dinosaur Valley State Park in Somervell County ... right outside of Glen

Nice to make your acquaintance,
Dr. Carl Baugh

Rose, *the town we'd be moving to* in two months' time! Dr. Carl Baugh was his name.

Now Carolyn is particularly interested Biblical apologetics, archeology, dinosaurs, and how it all comes together in the Creation story. So, we upped the volume and were fascinated with Dr. Baugh's compelling story of *dinosaur* tracks being discovered in the same geological strata as man's footprints — and how *that* all fits perfectly with the Biblical account of Creation. Dr. Baugh's persuasive presentation was fascinating, intriguing, and way over our heads … but we knew, once we got to Glen Rose, we would have to go to his museum and meet the man. We later found out this learned paleontologist had given lectures in over twenty-two countries over many years, sharing his knowledge and insight on how things all came into existence and stay together on the planet we call home.

Fast forward a few months, and there we sat in the Creation Evidence Museum with scores of other people listening to Dr. Baugh explain his Biblical and scientific understanding of Creation, The Fall, The Great Flood, The Ark, dinosaur footprints, Ice Age, and so much more. Once again, it was beyond us, but I was thinking, "*I'm sure glad he's on our side.*" I'm a believer.

During the program, Dr. Baugh explained how an atmospheric "canopy" that had covered the earth since the beginning of time had collapsed several thousands of years ago, and that The Flood had come and destroyed all living things on Earth (Noah and family and animals in the Ark were the exceptions). The earth's magnetic field had been altered, and that changed much about life as we know it here on earth.

Among other things, that led to Dr. Baugh segueing into discussion of how the poison/venom found in various vipers and certain insects today can be *neutralized* by an electrical shock administered quickly at the site of a bite. He pulled out a small device that looked somewhat like a cigarette lighter, but in reality, was a small "stun gun" of sorts. He explained, for example, that if used properly, this brief shock could be very useful for counteracting poisonous snake/insect bites on humans, farm animals, and even some pets. I'm thinking, "Hey, we'll be living out in the country soon … maybe one of those might come in handy someday."

Dr. Baugh told the story of walking through a rain forest in New Guinea years earlier with several fellow scientists doing some exploration and archeological research when he was stung by a large, venomous hornet on his left arm. His arm went immediately numb and limp. Because he was carrying his "gun," he quickly administered two to three quick shocks; and within a minute or so, the feeling in his arm returned. Voila!

So, after giving the audience a fair and proper disclaimer (he'd been demonstrating this for years) that this procedure is not a cure and should be used only in emergencies, and to be sure to follow printed instructions, etc. Dr. Baugh then asked if there was *anyone* in the audience that would like to try this on themselves (with his monitoring, of course). Not me ... but my brave Carolyn! Yep, she took him up on it front and center of everyone and did great. Said it felt like a brief, just below-the-skin tingling electrical shock — exactly what it was.

So, we decided to get one for the family (just in case). We were able to acquire this small stun gun in a neighboring community (for medical use by veterinarians) and felt we needed to show our elementary-aged kids how this would work if necessary. Nothing to be scared of, just to demonstrate in person for their benefit. We popped in the battery, and Carolyn volunteered to be first. She'd already been through this with Dr. Baugh. I'd shock her, then she'd shock me. She extended her arm right out there, I zapped her — and she shrieked and almost slapped me! Whoa! It hurt big-time, and *I was the culprit.* At first, I thought she was kidding. Uh oh, guess it was my turn then, and Carolyn couldn't wait. She did the deed ... and I let out a yelp that could be heard to kingdom come. My kids scattered outta that room lickety-split and went into hiding ... until they were assured — *no more stunning!*

Well, as the adults in the room, we should have known better. *Always read the directions first!* We should have noted: to test the device "in-air" first, set it at a low level of intensity, know how long to keep in contact with the skin, and the proper amount of pressure to be applied, etc. My new motto became: *"When all else fails, follow instructions."* Fortunately, we

never had the need to try out our
Pocket Guard neutralizer. My .410
shotgun became my go-to device to
keep vermin at bay.

P.S. Though my wife and I have
seen and greeted Dr. Baugh briefly
in passing in town over the years, I did have the distinct pleasure of having
lunch with this eighty-six-years-young consummate gentleman a few weeks
back. What a humble intellect and research scientist he is! What a soothing
inviting voice the Good Lord has given him as well — no wonder he's been
in radio and TV all these years! We had a great laugh and fellowship together
as I recounted our family's fun stun gun story. After the privilege of really
meeting him, I'm even more glad he's on our side. Amen!

# 15

# STARRY, STARRY FRIGHT

So, there we were, wife Carolyn and I, all settled in our new "gravity chairs" out on the back patio, taking in the starry sky one recent spring evening. Now, we live in the country and have gazed many a time over the years at the beautiful nighttime sky and countless stars and constellations across the universe. But this night was going to be special — we had just gotten these chairs (retreads from Goodwill) for just such an occasion, and there was actually supposed to be a grand display of meteor showers in the heavens if we timed it just right.

These so-called "gravity chairs" are new to me. They're somewhat cumbersome to get in and out of if one's not familiar with how they work, and I was not. But once you get the hang of it, one can see how they'd be perfect for our purpose that night ... but still. We were about two feet apart, got all reclined and comfy, and staring upwards. Since my cataract surgery last year, I've been able to see clearly at a distance (without glasses) for the first time in some sixty years. And what a sight to behold! As believers in the Maker of Heaven and Earth, we couldn't help but lie there in awe of His handiwork, His majesty, His omnipotence (Psalm 8). And to think, He put all that up there for us to enjoy, to appreciate, and to recognize!

It turned just a little cloudy this particular night, but the stars were still bright. We were still... and all was quiet. In our relaxed supine position, we even wondered aloud if one specific shining star, slightly to the right of the crescent moon, might be Mars? It did seem to have a *reddish* tint of a sparkle as it flashed its twinkle for all the earth to see. Not sure, but it was fun to imagine, that if it is, in fact, *Mars* (and we live long enough), we might actually see (via advanced camera technology) astronauts walk on that celestial surface someday. Some sixty million miles from earth! Through the intermittent clouds, we also seemed to spot a couple clusters of constellations and wonder ... just wonder.

We were in the midst of that silent, serene, reflective moment, when all of a sudden Carolyn let out a frightening scream that shattered the tranquility of the night. Not one scream, mind you, but a series of short screams as she struggled to get out of her chair. Totally startled by her shrieks, I clumsily scrambled trying to get out of my uncooperative chair — and be the brave, protective man she married! I must have looked more like Barney Fife flailing in the air trying to escape some type of rope trap. Some help I was, as Carolyn kept screaming, shaking, and needing my reassuring hug. Finally, I tumbled sideways out of the chair (now that's a trick), and grabbed her close. What!? What!? What was it!? A snake, big spider, a raccoon?! An alien? What!?

Carolyn expressed in scared, breathy short sentences — she didn't know, she didn't know. But that there was this cold, wet, large nuzzle type-thing that came up out of the dark from nowhere and made solid contact with her left shoulder and started to lick her! The culprit? One of our not-so-near neighbor's free-roaming Great Pyrenees that had been wandering the area for the last several months. Yeah, "Ol' Romeo" had been on the loose alright. Another neighbor on the other side of us had told us of this dog that had recently hooked up with their female Great Pyrenees mix and will be a "Daddy Dog" in a few weeks. No wonder it was roaming. The thing is, Romeo seems to be a sweet dog okay and was just standing there and probably only looking for companionship.

After the shock wore off and we calmed down a bit, we couldn't help but be kind to this gentle creature and pet it for a minute or two. Still, we didn't want to get anything started. We didn't want this happening again! After that adrenaline surge, neither one of us was in a particular mood

"Romeo" on the prowl

for anymore stargazing for the night. Carolyn was ready to call it a night. Just as well … being the brave, protective, proud husband I am, I needed to change out of my slightly-dampened pajama pants anyway — you know … *Tinkle, Tinkle … No matter who you are.*

# 16

# ELEMENTARY SCHOOLMATES CONNECT AFTER FIFTY-FIVE YEARS AND ONE THOUSAND MILES APART

A few years ago, my wife Carolyn and I were privileged enough to acquire a small get-away place in East Tennessee. Now we both love Texas, but there's just something about the mountains, rivers, trees, and waterfalls that beckons us to that area of our great country ever so often. Adding to the allure, Carolyn actually grew up in Middle Tennessee, and I have some ancestral roots from up that way (my grandfather, Charles Sr., was born in Bristol, Tennessee). So, we have that connection.

Shortly after getting settled in our little house, I tuned in to the clearest and strongest radio signal I could find – Super Talk 92.9 FM (Conservative Talk Radio) in the Tri-Cities area of Johnson City, Bristol, and Kingsport, Tennessee. I'm lying in bed one early morning half asleep and I hear this guy, George West, come on the air for "The George West Morning Show." He had a somewhat folksy vernacular ... yet his voice was clear, strong, and soothing at the same time. Though not as polished, aggressive, or assertive as the local pros I'm used to hearing in the DFW Metroplex, George was still very knowledgeable. He easily connected with listeners who'd call in and yet still be deferential with those in his listening audience who might have an opposing view. I actually found that quite refreshing.

So, this particular day, I'm listening to ol' George, and he said something like this, "Yeah, I have great memories of my growing-up years out in West Texas. Now East Tennessee is my home and boy, do I love it here … lots. But I'm very fond of my early years out in Odessa and Midland — great/honest hardworking people, beautiful sunsets, good schools, and a genuine sense of community. Love 'em both." What?! Here I am in bed at 6:15 in the morning listening to this guy on the radio broadcasting in the midst of beautiful Tennessee mountains talking about growing up in and loving, of all places, my hometown of Odessa, Texas. Now, if you know West Texas, you know what I'm a-talkin'-about.

I'm thinking, I gotta go meet this guy. So, I called the station up after he was off the air, and we connected. We had a brief, cordial phone conversation and agreed to do lunch sometime when I'm back in the area. It took a few months for all the logistics to work out, and by this time George had actually moved to another radio station. Still, he suggested for us to do a sack lunch together at his new station, and we could get acquainted during his frequent breaks off air. Fair enough. And get acquainted we did — my goodness! We find out that though he's four years younger than me, we both attended Austin Elementary School *together* in Odessa in the years 1960-61. We both learned to read and write in the very same building some fifty-five years earlier! I was in the fifth grade and he was in the first — yeah for the Fightin' Blue and Gold! We both love early Beatles music, Tex-Mex, Furr's Cafeteria, Friday Night Lights football, and the Monahans Sandhills (thirty miles west of Odessa). He had an uncle who was the sheriff over in Monahans, and I had a college roommate from there. We discovered that over the years, not only had we lived in Odessa at the same time, but at one time or another we'd both lived in the Dallas-Fort Worth area, Chicago, and Houston.

Later George asked me if, when I was of age, did I ever go out to the honky-tonk dance clubs in Odessa called "The Melody Club" and "The Stardust Club." I hem-hawed around a bit before confessing, "Well, I did that *one* time." George just laughed, and said his daddy used to sing and play guitar in a band there and worked as a front man/manager of sorts for both clubs over the years in the early '60s. George's dad also had a live Country Western TV show on weekends on KOSA TV in Odessa. "Big-Time" … well, not really. But I guess *it* was for his dad. I know *my daddy* must have seen George's dad on TV on those regular Saturday afternoon shows. My dad liked tuning in to those shows on weekends. Who'd ever "thunk" that?

Then his daddy got right with the Lord and *that changed everything.* He left the night club scene, bought three radio stations in the Midland/Odessa area, and became a preacher. Funny how that works. That's how my new friend George got into radio. His daddy offered him a chance to cut his teeth as a DJ at a little ol' station in little ol' Crane, Texas. Heady stuff for mid-teenager. "You know Crane, Texas, Charlie?" "Do I know Crane, Texas!? Why that's the home of the Fightin' Golden Cranes." We both just had to laugh and knew we were starting to connect on a deeper level. George got some experience there in Crane, then moved on up to doing some DJ work in the larger market of nearby Odessa on KOZA Radio. He became quite well-known in the area … so much so that the iconic national radio man "Wolfman Jack" even accepted George's invitation to come to Odessa to do a show. During their time together, George asked Wolfman what his secret was in having success in radio. In his distinct, gravelly voice, Wolfman replied, "Just 'lovezz de' people, George. Just 'lovezz de' people." It was an epiphany for the young aspiring DJ. He started applying that philosophy in his work, and his career took off and took him to major markets the land over.

Carolyn and I have had the privilege of getting to know George and his sweet wife Tina these last several years. Once early on, when we were guests

Black pepper on cantaloupe? Yee-haw!

over at their house for dinner, fresh cantaloupe was served as a side dish. When George asked me to pass the salt *and pepper* for the melon, I knew then "we waz true West Texas brethren." But of all the things George and I have in common, the greatest, most significant, wonderful of all, is our bond and mutual love for the Lord Jesus Christ. For both George and I, it was beyond those adolescent years, when the storms and trials of life came, that we were drawn to the Savior, thereby sealing our friendship. And one that will last a lot longer than fifty-five years, but through eternity! We'd say it was Providential.

# 17

# THANK GOD FOR
# THE SAFETY

When I was about ten years old, my parents entered my name in a drawing to win a .410 shotgun at the local Sears and Roebuck store there in Odessa. Of all things, my name was drawn! First and only thing like that I ever remember winning. Of course, I was too young to handle the gun properly, but it was good to have for the future and keep in the family. For over sixty years I've had some, but not much, experience with rifles, shotguns, revolvers, and pistols. I have mixed emotions about them.

But I do have stories. For instance, we had a BB gun around the house, and it was fun to shoot. I mainly just shot at cans, trees, and cardboard boxes I'd set up around in the yard. Once, I aimed at a sparrow high up in a neighbor's tree and shot that bird right in the head. It fell to the ground, and my excitement for being such a good shot soon morphed into one of remorse for killing an innocent little bird … remember "Opie" killing a mother bird with his slingshot? Well, that was me.

My folks used to go visit friends out in the country a few miles southwest of Odessa. These friends had a son they called "Bubba," probably age thirteen at the time, and a couple years older than me. They gave us each .22 rifles to go jackrabbit hunting, with the instructions to "be sure to be careful." They explained it was a good thing to kill those rabbits, because they carry disease, eat up what little vegetation there is out there for other animals, and were beginning to over-populate the area. So, we felt justified to shoot as many as we could find.

One time I'll never forget. We'd just started out, and Bubba was to my left and up in front of me about ten feet. Sure enough, a jackrabbit darted from behind a mesquite tree on my right and ran right across in front of me. Impulsively, I raised my rifle to shoot as I followed the rabbit from right to left, and I pulled the trigger. Nothing. *NOTHING!* Providentially, the gun did *not* fire — the safety was on. I would have shot my friend right in the back! He never knew of this; I had nightmares for years, and the incident haunts me to this day. I told no one.

Shortly thereafter, I went with my mom while she visited an older lady friend out in the country. Again, I had a .22 with me and just milled around the old farm house looking for things to shoot at. Soon I spotted a bunny rabbit run into a nearby bush. I quietly and slowly made my way there stalking my game and spotted it hiding under the bush a few feet away. I took careful aim and shot it straight on. Once again, my excitement for being such a good hunter transformed into regret, as I pulled the remains of a bloody cottontail out from the underbrush. That really wasn't much fun after all. Made me sad actually.

A year or so later, I was visiting my cousin Paul and his family outside Littlefield, Texas. They too lived in the country, and my Uncle Ned gave us each a small .22 Remington pistol to target practice with, so long as we agreed to "be extra careful." Ten minutes later, I let out a kind of scream like I'd never screamed before. Somehow, I'd gotten my left-hand ring finger over the front end of the barrel of the little gun, and it went off. It almost blew my finger off. Fortunately, the relatively small bullet went right through my finger, slightly below the top knuckle. God was with me that day, and the ER doctor was able to treat me so as to not lose my finger or part of it — which obviously could have had long-term ramifications. As a kid, you just don't think of those things. Nightmares again. I still have the 1/4-inch scar to prove it.

One of my dad's favorite pastimes was hunting. Not much to hunt out in West Texas, except for doves and rabbits; but he especially loved the challenge of bird hunting, so that's what he did. One time, during my college years, he took me dove hunting about an hour's drive southwest of Odessa. He gave me a double-barreled shotgun, and we set out for the stock tank, where my dad knew the doves would soon be flying in ... within a few minutes' time, here came the birds. I raised my gun and shot two times. Got a dove each time. My dad was very proud of and for me. Me, not so much. We walked over to retrieve the birds, and I watched him wring their necks, toss the heads aside, and put the dove in his shoulder pouch. I thought "I'm done." To my dad's credit and other true hunters' passion, he always, always never killed just to kill. He'd take his game home, clean it, and use it for food for the family or giveaway. I get that, and I don't begrudge other hunters — it's just not my game. Nor my meal.

I guess the first time I knew I was a real "softie" is when I took a good friend's eight- and ten-year-old daughters out for an afternoon movie back in 1976. I offered to do this, just as a favor, so he and the wife could have a nice lunch out and afternoon together. Well, "Bambi" was showing ... it had been decades since I'd seen "Bambi," and I had sorta forgotten how it all went. Then it started to hit me ... Uh oh. I remember now. So, the shots rang out, and there I am crying, holding on to these two adolescent girls who are trying comfort *me*. Not Good! Embarrassed? A little. Did I get over it? Pretty much. But I'm telling you, I ain't gonna go see "Bambi" again anytime soon ... That's my story on guns and killing. (One reason I like fishing so much is, after the thrill of catching who knows what, you can always just toss it back in for another day of fun/challenge).

Me and my trusty .410

P.S. Oh yes, I still have that .410 shotgun and have used it successfully and unabashedly on occasion out at my house in the country. Rattlesnakes and copperheads enter my domain on their own risk, and I'm at the ready to send them to "a better place." And I don't clean 'em for vittles either. I leave 'em be — that's for the vultures. It's their specialty.

# *18*

# REMEMBERING MY DADDY

My dad would have turned one-hundred-years-old on June 17, 2022, and I can't help but think what a tremendous influence he had on my life. Though he's been gone some sixteen years now, there's probably not a day that goes by that he doesn't cross my mind … probably several times. Despite our few times of strong disagreements and a couple of relatively short periods of noncommunication – the details of those hard memories seem so insignificant now and are rightfully fading away with time – the good, fatherly, supporting, and encouraging words and moments from him are what I recall much more readily and easily.

I realize for some people, it's just the other way around. So, I feel very fortunate and count my blessings. I'm also finding it's difficult to rid myself of some of the material things I inherited from him. I mean, I've got some whitish/silver "New Balance" brand walking shoes of his that I still wear on occasion to this day. When I put them on, I treat them gingerly, knowing his feet were right where mine are. Got his DNA in there. And for some weird reason, I feel I stand a little

One handsome
high school dude

taller, a little safer, a little more confident with them on. I know. I know. I've also got some ostrich leather cowboy boots of his that don't fit just right, but I still put 'em on anyway and wear them with pride and fond remembrance.

Of course, there's his old tools, watches, paintings, and furniture — things I can't seem to part with, and so I plan to pass them on to my kids one day. They probably won't need or have a use for those things, but I don't want to know that … not now anyway. Maybe you understand.

I have to tell you that Charles Jr. was by no means a saint. He had a tendency to be gruff, volatile, and a fuddy-duddy — character traits I was determined not to possess as I was growing up. Know what? To my chagrin, sometimes I'm just like him … *like father, like son*, I guess. (The good Lord still has work to do on me in those areas and more.)

Later on in my own life, I came to understand my father better too … especially as I matured and became more aware of things he went through. He had really tough times growing up in the Depression, became severely ill while in the Army Air Corp fighting in the Pacific during WWII, and lost his firstborn at childbirth (two and one-half years before I came around). From those revelations came empathy and a better understanding of who my dad was and why he was the way he was. That growing maturity gave me a desire and more of a willingness to extend grace and forgiveness to him, despite his reticence to seek it.

My father taught me the importance of being punctual and of being honest and generous to those less fortunate. He also had a gentle, caring, loving way with pets and animals. I think I have that. The thing is, he didn't preach all these things to me — he lived them out in front of me, and I adopted them as my own. In these sixteen years since his passing, I frequently think of questions I should have asked him. Like how I wished I'd have asked him more about my big sister Adele who died at childbirth and whom I never knew. And how did he and Mom get through those sorrowful days? What's the best memory he had of his own mother? His dad? Did he make good friends with any "Yankees" during his years in the War. What was the most fun thing he ever did with Mom, before and after marriage? What was it like in Odessa when Odessa High School won the state championship in football in 1946? Was there any one thing I did or said growing up that made him especially proud of me? Questions, questions ... questions I'll never know the answers to until I reunite with him in heaven someday. So ... *"Dad, I'm writing this piece to honor you. For I know you loved me unconditionally ... no matter anything. I also want you to know I'm very proud to bear your name and be Charles III. Always. I miss you, Daddy."*

Proud to be Charles III

To the reader: I'm writing this for you, too. If you have a parent that is still alive, endeavor to ask questions. Dig deep if you dare, but only if they're willing to talk. Probe gently and in love and you might find there are stories in them you know not of. You'll never regret it. For when they're gone, the stories go with them.

P.S. I've been driving my dad's old 2000 Toyota Avalon since I inherited it from him in 2007. It's been my main car all these years, got 348,000 miles on it, and countless memories in it. One day, in the not-too-distant future, I'll be giving her up ... and I know I will need to have a couple of facial tissues on hand.

*I traded in the Avalon for a Supersonic Red 2022 Toyota Camry. RED for Odessa High's colors ... and took possession of this new car (ordered ten months previously) on July 6, 2022 – the day I turned seventy-two! Great birthday gift!*

# 19

# MOMMY MIGHT BE SINGING A DIFFERENT TUNE

Thirteen years ago, I retired from my job as a Flight Attendant with a major airline after thirty-four years. It was a terrific job for me and was a great fit for my personality. I love to travel, meet folks from all over, and be of service while on the job. Now there was always certain airline protocol we were taught to follow during our six weeks of training at Flight Attendant School. We F/As were expected to adhere to these guidelines and procedures no matter the situation. That was just the understanding between the company and its employees, and I always tried to be a "good boy" and do what was expected. Nevertheless, with the airline industry ever-changing and clientele much different from the mid '70s when I took the job, I became more and more comfortable interjecting my personality into my work and pushing the envelope a bit when deemed appropriate, a little on out there the last few years of my airline career.

So, it was one day, when I was on board our Super 80 aircraft at the gate (before passengers were boarded), preparing the galley area in the rear of the plane, when I was introduced to twelve-year-old "Abigail." She was what we called a UM (unaccompanied minor), and traveling by herself on her way to see her grandma. She was a "pre-board," and the agent who accompanied her toward the back of the aircraft made sure I knew of her presence and was properly introduced. Standard protocol.

So, as I'm getting things organized for our in-flight service, little Abby pipes up "Whatcha doing?" Well, right off I could tell this girl was smart, inquisitive, and outgoing. So, I told her I was preparing the galley and cart for the beverage/snack service we would be doing about twenty minutes after takeoff. She wanted to know about all my tasks, the airplane, etc. Not at all a pest but just a curious adolescent spreading her wings, and I liked that. As we talked more, I thought, you know, maybe little Abby would like to work the cart with me on our beverage service. I can show her all she needs to know, and I'll be right there with her the whole time (I'd done this with my own daughter a couple of times years before, and it worked out just fine).

My fellow F/A who usually worked with me back in the Main Cabin could help out in First Class and could assist us in the back if need be. So, I asked Abby if she would like to work with me on the cart when it was time to serve the passengers and safe to do so. She said she'd love to. We took off, and when the time came, Abby got out of her seat, and I showed her the ropes. Then I thought, you know this young lady might enjoy helping me make the inflight PA, informing our customers to try to stay clear of the aisle as they best can during our service, what items/beverages we have to offer, etc. I would tell her what to say. She said, "I'm all in." Good, this could be fun!

So, I told her that it was time to make our announcement and to just repeat what I told her to say. "Okay?" "Okay!" I pulled little

My workplace for 34 years

Abby over close to me and the intercom/microphone and held the "speak" button down continuously as I began the introduction: "Ladies and Gentleman, we'll be beginning our inflight beverage service in the main cabin momentarily. Today, I have with me a very special helper. Her name's Abby. She's going to be working with me on the cart. Say 'hello' to everybody, Abby." "Hello, everybody." Good. "Now Abby, what are we able to offer these fine folks to drink off of our cart?" I pointed to various items, and she just named 'em off: "We got Cokes, Sprite, Ginger Ale, orange juice, water, coffee, etc." She did really well. Then I said, "We also have a few snack items for sale, like Lay's Stack potato chips and Grandma's cookies. These items are how much, Abby?" I held up three fingers, and she said, "$3." Right! We went through the whole spiel together, efficiently and smoothly, and Abby seemed like a little pro at this. The whole time I've had my thumb down on the phone's "speak" button so the passengers could actually hear my interaction with Abby.

Finally, it just came to me to say, somewhat in jest, "And *we accept* tips!" (Definitely NOT airline protocol). Well, I wasn't expecting this — Abby's demeanor immediately changed, and she responded in a whiney, girly, adolescent voice on the PA: "YOU'RE not supposed to take tips!" Caught me totally off-guard. Surprising even myself, I retorted with, "Who said we're not supposed to take tips?!" "Mommy said you're NOT supposed to take tips!" I paused a couple of seconds trying to think, and then I just came out with: "Well, guess what, Little Sister … Mommy's not on this plane, is she?" "No, sir." "So, who do you think is in charge of this service back here?" "You are." "Right!" "Any more questions?" "No, sir." "Got it?" "Got it!" Then I smiled at her with a thumbs up sign, and we were all good. So, with that all settled, I proceeded to obtain an extra "airsickness bag," folded down the sides and marked in big letters "*NON-SOLICITED TIPS*" and plopped it down on top of our cart for full viewing as we made our way with up and down the aisle. Abby did a great job, and I'll say, engaged her customers better than a few of fellow employees I'd worked with in years past. The thing is, Abby happily walked off the plane about $25 richer than when she walked on. Not many passengers can say that, and maybe Mommy changed her tune.

## 20

# FAMOUS "MICKEY" WAS REGULAR "MIKE" TO ME

Back in the winter of 1978, I had transferred to the Washington, D.C. area from Chicago as a relatively new employee of American Airlines. I was a Flight Attendant, and my newly appointed supervisor was a fellow named Mike Kuhn. When I met Mike, right off I liked him — he was professional, yet easy going. Personable, yet knew his stuff. Mike was about eighteen years my senior but treated me with respect as the young adult I was; and I respected him for that. Mike was just somebody you could talk to, and all my co-workers felt that with Mike onboard, we were working toward the same goal of making AA an even better airline (and having a decent income as well).

The thing is, it wasn't until months later that I find out Mike was a celebrity of sorts in his "previous life" as child actor "Mickey Kuhn" in the late '30s, '40s, and '50s. Really. In fact, here was a guy I had actually seen on the big screen some ten years earlier in Dallas when the iconic movie "Gone with The Wind" was re-released to the nation for the first time in a decade (1968). Who'd have ever "thunk" that? Yessir, he was in a couple of scenes with Clark Gable (Rhett) and Vivien Leigh (Scarlett) as her nephew "Beau Wilkes" and son of Ashley and Melanie Wilkes. Mickey was six years-old at the time, and with Olivia De Havilland's passing a couple of years ago in Paris at age 104, Mickey/Mike is now the last surviving cast member from Gone with The Wind — the epic Civil War drama of life in the Antebellum South of the 1860s. The 1939 movie won ten Academy Awards, including "Best Picture."

But you know what's great about Mike? Mike's just a regular guy who's friends to regular people. One would not know of his celebrity status unless one delves deeper into this good man's life. Mike also has the distinction of being the only cast member from GWTW to have appeared in a later film with Vivien Leigh — "A Street Car Named Desire." He does remember Mr. Gable as being especially nice to him and Miss Leigh as someone who took him in and helped him feel at ease when filming his part. Hattie McDaniel was especially kind to Mike. So, he has fond memories. Over the years he continued to stay in touch with Miss DeHavilland via phone, letters, and emails until just a few years ago.

In 1979, I moved on from Washington, D.C. to Nashville, and Mike moved to Boston in mid-management with AA. Whenever in Boston, usually just passing through, I'd seek out my friend there at the airport, and we'd have a chance to catch up and exchange niceties. But then I retired and lost touch until about nine years ago. Through a little research I was able find a contact and reconnect with Mike. He and his wife Barbara live in Florida in the winters/spring and then head up to the Boston area for the summers/ fall. A blessed life he's had, and he knows it. Wife Carolyn and I had

Jefferson, TX – spring 2022

a chance to have dinner with Mike and his wife when we took a trip to the Northeast one autumn a few years back. How beautiful and historic that part of our country is! At age eighty-seven, Mike's had some health issues but still gets along quite okay and feels very blessed and grateful for all the things he's been able to do in his storied life. But regardless of his notoriety, I'd choose to be his friend anyway. The way the world is today, we'd all be better off if we could be like Mike.

*Mike Kuhn passed away at the age of 90 in November 2022. I was very privileged to know Mike, and my life was a little fuller because of it.*

# *21*

# NEW BEGINNINGS FOR HEATHER

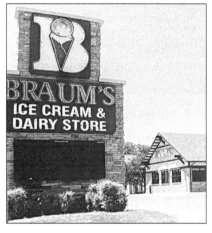

Last November I was driving through a neighboring community around lunchtime and had a hankering for a hamburger. I glanced up to see this eatery that was known for their good hamburgers. In my thirty years in the area, I'd never patronized this particular location. Behind the counter was a woman, probably in her mid-forties, ready to take my order. As she did, and in her personable, upbeat kind of way, I couldn't help but notice she was *missing perhaps half of her teeth* – and the ones she did have were darkly-stained and looked like they were rotting away. Yet this lady kept on communicating cheerfully with her co-workers and the next-in-line customers … as if nothing. I wondered *what in the world happened to* this woman? How did she (or anyone) get this way?

As I was eating my lunch, I kept thinking about the woman behind the counter. Then, then … there was this inner prompting that seemed to say, *"You are to help that woman."* At first, I just dismissed the thought. But the notion came on again, only stronger. As a believer in the Maker of heaven and earth, I sensed the Good Lord was directing me reach out to this person

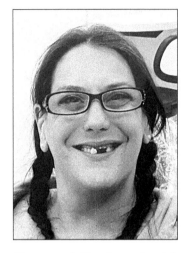

in need. *"This is my charge to you."* Oh my... I don't normally experience such a "spiritual" nudging quite so clearly as I did at that moment. Where to begin?

Well, I am an organizer, so my first thought was to talk inconspicuously to her boss and get a little information about the woman. I was able to have the manager, "Patricia," discreetly come over to me, and I gently inquired about the counter lady. She carefully shared with me a few things about Heather. Heather's punctual and dependable, a good worker who gets along with most everybody; but a number of years ago, she'd made some poor life decisions and got into methamphetamine. But Patricia quickly pointed out that Heather's been "clean" for over two years now and would probably love for someone to help her with what would be major dental work. Patricia told me she would talk with Heather on my behalf and see if she'd be open to someone like me (a total stranger) helping her, and then we'd be in touch again in a few days with Heather's response.

In the meantime, I knew a fellow churchgoer in my Sunday School Class who is a retired dentist. I thought he'd be a great resource for me to better understand what I might be getting myself into. Ron was the guy, and from my description to him of Heather's condition, he told me she most likely had what is known as "Meth Mouth." I inquired what possibly could be done, where I could go, and approximately how much this endeavor might cost. Ron gave me the lowdown and suggested I might start with The Texas A&M School of Dentistry in downtown Dallas — a very well-respected, first-class facility with certified doctors/ professional staff, and most likely quite reasonable costs to the patient. I called the school and listened to a recording on how to get signed up for an appointment for an evaluation/initial exam. The school was out of session for the holidays but would start taking appointments December 12 at 10:00 a.m. sharp for next semester (opening slots for new patients fill up very quickly).

So, a few days later I called Heather's boss, Patricia, and asked if she'd had time to talk with Heather about my thoughts. "Oh, yes. She would like that very much and would love to meet you and discuss the possibilities." Within a few days I went back to the hamburger place and met Heather for the first time in person. It was a sweet, emotional time, and she was willing to pursue with me this idea of getting her teeth all fixed up to help her have a new start in life. I made no promises on things quite yet but was willing to do my due diligence to do what I could. She assured me she's been off drugs for over two years, is trying to quit smoking, and really wants to start anew. I knew from this short meeting that the Good Lord had put me on to this for Heather's good and the greater good. So, I did get through to the School of Dentistry on the morning of December 12 for an appointment/evaluation/exam set for January 26.

Heather and I briefly touched bases a couple of times over the holidays, and then the big day came. We weren't even sure if they would take Heather as a patient, but we were going to take our chances. I picked her up at her house, and we headed off for the two-hour drive to Dallas. I told her to feel free to share with me only what she felt comfortable telling me and that I did not judge her on anything. I promised to just be a listening friend she could trust. She opened up to me freely and easily about her situation. She's forty-five-years-old, has been married a couple of times and is estranged from her current husband, has two young adult sons, and lives with her folks. She admits readily that she made some really poor choices early in life along the way and would love to have a "reset in life," if you will. I knew the Lord was using me as the catalyst to help make this happen. What a privilege!

Besides my wife Carolyn's and our monetary contribution, we obviously needed more funds (finding out later to be estimated to be between $6,000 – $7,000). Initially, I wrote a group email to about a dozen close friends telling them of Heather's story and the need for prayer and monetary donations if they felt so led. I also was able to mention this to my Sunday School Class at church and gave them a brief synopsis of my encounter with Heather and the need to raise the funds for her treatment. I tried to make known that any monetary gifts toward this end should not be in lieu of other ministry/church offerings, etc. My goodness, there are so many other people, missions, and charitable organizations that have pressing needs that I wanted to be careful to explain this situation wisely. That being said, we had about two dozen people donate generously to the cause, and we are now fully-funded.

But it's not only about the money but about deeper, spiritual issues as well. I've seen the unselfishness, the goodness in people's hearts — reaching out in total acceptance of a toothless Heather when she's visited our Sunday School Class. Embracing her just as she is. Loving her as the Good Lord sees her and exhorting us to love our neighbor as ourselves.

We're in the midst of seeing God change a life … and maybe others along the way because of her. That's what He does, you know. Heather has given up smoking and even brought her folks to church as an expression of her gratitude for the way and manner unknown people are helping her turn her life around … just doing what we're to be about.

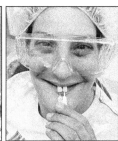

# HEATHER'S THOUGHTS

## *WHAT THE PAST YEAR HAS MEANT FOR ME ...*

*Everything! I never thought I would be where I am now.*

*My life was empty a year ago ... an ugly smile, struggling with hard relationships, and going through the pain of insecurity regarding my life and my appearance.*

*I had a job where I worked hard and smiled at everyone even though my smile wasn't pretty. It was a smile I always gave freely, but I never wanted it to be seen in pictures.*

*Then Charlie came into my life and things changed. He saw something in me that I did not know even existed ... most importantly he led me to my new relationship with God. If it were not for Charlie and the many others who joined him in supporting me, I wouldn't be where I am today. I can see how much I have grown as a person in the last year, and I am ready to smile my true smile again.*

*Heather C.*

Heather's baptism

**Turn the page for a photo collage of Heather's journey!**

# Abbreviated Pictorial Collage of Heather's Journey

# 22

# CATCHING A "WHOPPER" AT CAMP

Some sixty years ago, I remember a time when summer meant I'd be going off to YMCA Camp Carter on the outskirts of Fort Worth for a couple of weeks. Yep, I'd happily leave my comfortable, secure home in Odessa in anticipation of adventure and outdoor fun at summer youth camp with 150 other boys. Who knew what experiences, life lessons, and interesting people would be coming my way?

I went to camp three years there as a preadolescent, and each time I came back home a little more mature and the better for it. My dad would drive the two of us the six hours there and we'd talk ... him mostly. I distinctly remem-

ber when I was probably eleven or twelve, my dad, while in the car driving, casually brought up the subject of *SEX* to me. I was quite unawares and naïve, and he told me stuff I'd never heard of before ... yuck! I was *more concerned* with having enough earthworms for fishing in the camp's small lakes than I was of the birds and bees. That said, and his knowing of my great desire to catch a "whopper," my dad had packed away a small cardboard tub of night crawlers in the car trunk for just that purpose.

At camp, I learned lots of things. At registration, each kid was assigned a counselor and a cabin that had five or six bunk beds. There were probably ten or twelve fellow campers in my cabin, "Choctaw" Cabin, one year. The next year, it was "Cherokee," and so on. I liked sleeping on the top level of my bunk — you could get away from the rigors of camping up there if you wanted. Sometimes, even when the lights were out, I'd slip out my trusty transistor radio (on the sly) and catch a few innings of my beloved Houston Colt .45s… getting beat once again. (A year or two later, the team was renamed the Houston Astros.) They were awful. Still, I loved that team — the only pro baseball team in Texas at the time.

At the rifle range I learned gun safety and how to be a better shot with a .22 rifle, and I qualified as a "Junior Marksman." We did crafts, horseback riding, and canoeing too. If you were good enough in canoeing class, you might be selected to go on an overnight canoe trip on the Brazos River. My last year there, I was determined to go on that trip. So, I tried extra hard and became quite good at rowing, turns, etc. I was certain I'd be chosen. Alas, the last spot went to the son of one of the camp directors. Hard lessons for a young whippersnapper like me to learn in that situation. The lessons — "life just ain't fair sometimes" and "it's *who* you know more than *what* you know." One of my first exposures to "politics" in what was supposed to be a carefree, buoyant camp experience. I was learning things alright. Still, it was a great time. It was a growing-up time for me, and I'm thankful for the experience.

We had to write short letters to our folks twice a week, and I know my parents got a kick out of my mentioning I had to do "KP" duty (Kitchen Patrol) every other day at the dining hall. At KP, I learned teamwork, responsibility, and in a strange kind of way, the satisfaction "work" can bring in doing a good job for a purpose.

Now about fishing — that was a success! I once caught a three-to-four-pound bass from the little lake in front of the mess hall on an artificial lure. First time ever had I done something like that! The problem was I didn't

Site of both of my catches

know what to do with my great catch. Someone suggested, I ought to give it to one of the cooks at the mess hall. So, I did and the sweet, large Black lady (terrific cook by the way) I gave it to was most appreciative … *but*, the biggest thing I ever caught in my three years I went there? Another camper! Not good. Yes sir, hooked him right smack in his forearm while carelessly casting my lure. Boy, did I feel bad about that. Almost made me sick. That's when I learned what an "infirmary" was. The staff nurse took care of my fellow camper pretty easily, and I learned another life lesson: don't do that.

On Sunday mornings, we had a little chapel service at the small amphitheater nestled in the woods nearby. I heard and learned "Kum Ba Ya" for the first time there and felt a sense of peace in my little spirit that would grow into fruition about a decade later. So that was camp for me. My parents wanted me to grow up some while there (and I did), and to this day I'm appreciative for the opportunity they afforded me. Wonderful memories.

P.S. Oh yes, one other thing I learned during those camping days: *Never ever* leave your fishing worms in the trunk of your car in the blazing Texas sun in 100-degree temperature! We had inadvertently concocted our own stinkbait — "Baked Worms a la Cardboard Casserole." Eww-ee!

## 23

# FROM SINGER ON AN ALBUM
# TO FOREVER FRIEND

In 1975, I was a relatively new Christian working in my first job right out of college and living in Hawaii. I had grown up in West Texas and in the church, but I had never really grasped what it meant to "have a relationship with Jesus" vs. "having 'religion,' believing in God, and trying to be a good person." That is, until I was twenty-two-years-old and in dire need of new direction

Album that started it all for me

in my life that I confessed my sins and asked Jesus into my heart. My past church experience had been pretty much ho-hum. The music seemed so old-fashioned, with the same old choir in robes, singing the same old songs and accompanied by nothing other than a piano and organ. Ugh … the organ. Heaven forbid if there'd ever been a guitar or violin in the mix … much less a drum set. The one song I sorta liked was "Onward Christian Soldiers" — and even then, my daddy reprimanded me (ten years-old) for "marching" in place to the beat of the music. You get it.

Enter a new-found faith and new era of Christian music for young believers. This time, the mid 1970s, Contemporary Christian music was just emerging, and a whole new sound of music and interest in spiritual things swept across our land. It even became somewhat cool to be a "Jesus Freak." I didn't go that far, but I did love Jesus and embraced this new music that stirred my soul. So it was then that a former roommate of mine, David, told me about a fantastic new group "Dogwood" he'd been hearing fairly regularly at "Koinonia," a Christian coffee house in Nashville. "Man, are they talented!" "Dogwood" was a trio made up of a husband-and-wife team (Steve and Annie Chapman) and singer/guitarist Ron Elder. Steve wrote most of their songs, played guitar/banjo, and most times was the lead singer. Annie had a wonderfully pleasing, strong voice, would take the lead on occasion, and could harmonize with the best of 'em. And Ron was a singer/guitarist, an all-around talent, and the perfect complement to their unique sound.

Anyway, I got their first album and loved it. I'd never heard anything quite like this. Their music and the lyrics in their songs hit me in the heart … real life experiences and true stories of love and lost love, temptation, guilt, and faith, forgiveness and redemption. I became a fan from the get-go.

So it was, a couple years later, I was in a new job with the airline living on the outskirts of Chicago. A group of us young Christians went to hear a concert by popular singer B. J. Thomas (a fairly new believer himself) at a high school gymnasium a few miles southeast of the Windy City. The warm-up group for B.J? *Dogwood!* They came on stage, sang their songs, and I was hooked on more than a feeling. I liked them better than B.J., and I liked B.J. They sang truth with lyrics that touched my soul. And they lived in Nashville, the place where I'd been hoping to relocate to since joining the airline! Though it took patience, prayer, and a couple of years, I finally got my transfer there in April 1979.

Within a few weeks, I found myself frequenting the coffee house/bookstore at Koinonia; and one particular day while there, I recognized Steve

Chapman from across the way. I just had to introduce myself and tell him how much I appreciated his talent and his ways on stage. He was very appreciative, and humbled actually. So easy to talk to … just a down-to-earth, ordinary kinda guy, and *actually wanted to know about me*. So, we talked more and realized we had much in common. Both born in 1950, same conservative mindset, kindred sense of humor, and we both loved the Lord. We just clicked. For one thing, Steve was a big fan of The Andy Griffith Show. Like me, we felt "Barney Fife" made the show. That next Sunday, at Belmont Church (right across the street from Koinonia), I spotted Annie before the service began. I distinctly remember going up to her seated in the pew near the aisle, kneeling down and saying, "Annie, my name is Charlie. I met your husband last week at Koinonia, and I just wanted to tell you how much I love your music, and especially the way *you* sing. Your song 'I'll Bring Him Back to You' is so heart-felt, moving, and powerful." She was very gracious in her response, and I'm glad I introduced myself.

Shortly thereafter, Steve and I had lunch together and became real friends. He was a preacher's kid, and both he and Annie grew up in West Virginia. He gave up team sports in school for hunting and fishing and took up guitar and writing songs. After high school, he joined the Navy and became more aware of the worldly ways outside the protective canopy of involved parents, the church, and small-town West Virginia. His parents instilled in him the core values of a life lived for the Lord that remain the essence of his life to this day — honesty, faith, trust, confession, repentance, wisdom, hope, respect, honor, generosity, empathy … need I say more? I could easily go on.

Within the year of that first meeting Steve and Annie, Dogwood had pretty much run its course as a singing group. Steve felt his first priority was with his family (two little Chapman kids had come along), and touring was no longer feasible or practical. Sad for us fans, but right for them. Still Steve and I stayed in touch. He continued to write songs, all the time wondering,

"Maybe in a year or two, think anybody might be interested enough to come hear a man play guitar and sing songs with his wife?" The thing is, Steve is actually as good of a story-teller as he is a singer, and the down-to-earth lyrics of his songs penetrate the heart of

Steve and Annie – meant to be

the listener. For example, in one of their early songs, he addresses a couple on the verge of divorce when their little boy says/sings: *"Daddy, please find a reason to stay with my momma We both love you Please don't leave And if you can't find a reason, Daddy, I wouldn't mind If you want that reason to be me."* Poignant, convicting, Heaven-sent words. Annie could/and did handle the harmony parts and often the lead with aplomb and sweet sincerity that immediately connects with an audience … whether that audience be 40 or 4,000 in number. So that's what they decided to try. Because I sing like Barney Fife (regardless of voice lessons from Mrs. Poltice … not!), I "proposed" to Steve in jest maybe joining up with them and making it a trio again! Just kidding, of course. Still, maybe I *could* help the Chapmans get started in other ways. Maybe I could organize, promote, do a newsletter, propose ideas, or help in design on logo/stationery, make calls, whatever.

I mean, the price was right. I'm theirs for the taking. I believed in their talent and their purpose. Really, I just believed in them. I knew the Lord had given them a gift to be shared. So, as it was, I actually got to volunteer/ work for Steve and Annie Chapman for several years. It was a great honor to be a part of something/someone so very special — the two of them became known nationally as the "Musical Ambassadors for the Family" and were featured artists for Dr. James Dobson's 1985 film series "Turn Your Heart

Toward Home" (the song and title of the series Steve wrote). They appeared with Rev. Billy Graham in one of his crusades and were invited guest artists at the National Christian Booksellers Convention in Washington, DC, in 1986.

Proverbs 18:24 speaks of a friend who sticks closer than a brother. Though in real life I have no siblings, I found that friend and brother in Steve Chapman. An endearing/enduring friendship I count as a privilege to have. Who could have planned that a fellow singing on a record I first listened to some 4,300 miles away and forty-two years earlier would one day be one of my very closest friends? I know Who. We both serve Him.

Good buds in Tennessee (2019)

*Steve Chapman was an integral part of The Velvets Endeavor as described in story 7 and story 8 in this book. A constant anchor throughout the ever-changing plans we had in the works, Steve's wisdom, talent, and gift of time gave the city-wide event validity, professionalism, and spiritual depth necessary to do what we did in Odessa, Texas, in June 2022. I'm honored to call Steve my friend and brother.*

To learn more about Steve and Annie Chapman, their music, and ministry, go to **steveandanniechapman.com.**

## 24

# BIOLOGY TEACHER HAS STRANGE GENES

S ome teachers one never forgets. So, it is for me and Mr. Roger Corzine, my biology teacher during my sophomore year at Odessa High School in 1965. Mr. Corzine was in his mid-30s, wore distinctive horn-rimmed glasses, and was one mellow fellow. Everybody loved Mr. Corzine. You could just tell he was smart, but he was never intimidating... the kind of guy that just made you want to learn.

As I knew Mr. Corzine in class

Now, biology can be a tough subject alright. I had a particularly hard time going from identifying the various organs of a frog in our science book (so clearly displayed in the color transparencies) to the real organs we were to identify while dissecting a frog for a lab test. It didn't help matters that I got a little queasy when I sliced open my frog's abdomen for inspection ... whatever. But I studied hard and got an A in the course.

We did learn some really practical things in his class, though. For instance, we learned about the three types of blood cells we all have in common — red blood cells, white blood cells, and platelets. For those willing we'd have to make a blood smear. Using a standard simple finger prick (a small lancet tool dutifully supplied for each volunteer), we'd prick our own finger, smudge a droplet of blood on a glass slide and then observe the characteristics and numbers under a microscope for proper identification. I have to say, I'm not too keen on inflicting pain purposely on oneself. I've *never been into pain* too much. But I glanced over and saw these gals I've known since elementary school just-a-prickin' their fingers right along. Now I was used to seeing girls "primping" some, but not that! What's an aspiring athlete to do? Time to man up, Charlie Boy — I prick. It smarts. I bleed. I smudge. And I'm normal. Just glad I didn't have to lance myself again. That was not fun.

One cool dude, that Roger!

Another experiment we did in class: "Paul" and I were "volunteered" by our classmates to each take a petri dish, go out in the hall or even outside if so desired, and "kiss" the agar (the pinkish-colored gelatinous substance Mr. Corzine had placed in the bottom of the dish). We were supposed to give it a really good smooch too, and then return it to Mr. Corzine for safekeeping. Three days later we'd all be able to observe what, if any, bacteria/fungi had grown on the agar. So later that week, Mr. Corzine showed the class the two petri dishes. Paul's was nice, smooth, and hardly anything growing — just a perfect, intact lip imprint. Now I'm not sure of this, but I seem to recall he was awfully proud of himself. Ha! Not me. My petri dish agar had become all discolored with some kind of darkish moldy mildewy growth just-a-sproutin'. Everybody laughed, except me … actually, I think *that did something to my psyche* for years about my kissing the girls. Even worse, them toward me! Whatever. Over time, I guess I got over it, though it took a while. Let's just say, I *am* the proud grandfather of six grandkids, so it all worked out okay.

In class we also studied genetics and what the dominant traits were for various inherited characteristics. For instance, in humans, it might be hair color, hair texture, or eye color. For men in particular, it might show a propensity for baldness in the later years of life, etc. Anyway, we all did some study of dominant eye color probabilities and concluded that the brown gene was generally more dominant than the blue, etc., with some variations thrown in there. Toward the end of class one day, Mr. Corzine, standing front and center, said something like "Okay class, now that we've determined dominant traits for eye color, what would *you* say about someone that would have one eye one color and the *other* eye a different color?" We all piped up with things like "weird, strange, crazy, off, unnatural, eerie…" He seemed to go along with that, then promptly removed his glasses, opened his eyes wide and said "Well, what's that, again, you say you'd call this person?!" Sure enough, he had one *green* eye and one *blue* eye. We were all dumbfounded … never knew about those things before. But that's what Mr. Corzine was all about: teaching us kids scientific things alright, but also how learning can be fun, and how it's a good thing to think outside the box.

P.S. Mr. Corzine is ninety-three-years young now and still lives in Odessa. He and I reconnected after many years, and I've recently had the wonderful opportunity to visit him a couple times at his home and recall some fond memories of back in the day. Mr. Corzine happens to be the only person I know still around *who actually knew my grandfather*, Charles Sr. (1891 – 1964), back when they were both teachers at Odessa High in the mid-1950s. At seventy-three myself now, he allows me to call him "Roger." He could have moved on to other places after retirement. But he's been quite content in Odessa (been there since graduating from OU in 1952), and just feels at home there … because the people he knows and loves live in the area. He reminded me, "It's the people that make a place, Charlie. You can't befriend a tree. Trees don't hug back." Can't argue with that, "Rodge" …

Me and "Rodge," 59 years later as friends

Charles V "Chaz" meets
new friend who knew
Charles Sr. in the 1950s

# 25

# AND THE SECOND
# SHALL BE LAST

On Christmas Day 2020, we received the great news! Carolyn and I were going to be grandparents again. Our daughter Noelle and husband Zach had it all planned out — their little two-year-old son Ollie opened up the last present, a large Christmas-wrapped box (we grandparents thought it was going to be a big toy), and out floated blue and pink balloons with small cardboard signs attached, reading "Promoted to Big Brother." At 70 years-old at the time, it took me a moment to get it. But I finally got it, and what a thrill it was! Totally unexpected.

Our 35-year-old-son, Charles IV, already had four terrific boys (ages 9, 7, 5, 2), and he and wife Leigh are done. Noelle experienced some lingering medical issues after Ollie was born in October 2019; and even after full recovery, she informed us that she, too, was not planning on having any more kids. We understood and felt very blessed to have the five grandsons we've got — each one special in his own way. Yet, in the back of our minds, there was a little bit of a selfish yearning for Noelle to possibly change her mind once things settled down and, Lord willing, have one more.

Ollie needed a sibling (even if it's a girl ... ha!). So, as it was, if things went as planned, hoped and prayed, around the first week in August we'd have another little one as a part of our family. A few weeks after Christmas, there was scheduled a *reveal party* with two shooting canister flares of the colors blue or pink to indicate the gender. Noelle and Zach would each shoot them off simultaneously. As I was writing this story, nobody but Noelle's good friend Kathy (with the correct corresponding-colored flares in hand) knew if this little one was to be a boy or girl. We'd all find out the same time. I already had two boys' names and two girls' names all picked out and ready to submit for the "name suggestion" bowl. Noelle and Zach would be dutifully pulling out the small pieces of paper with the submitted names to read aloud for the gathering of friends and family. For me, I thought, hey, how about "Charles VI" or "Norman" for a boy's first name? And for a girl, I'm liking "Norma" or possibly "Noelle, Jr." … just saying. Actually, we were so pleased, it mattered not gender or name. We just knew we were so blessed.

I do/did ponder the kind of world these children would be growing up in, and it concerns me greatly. Most of us in our 60s, 70s, and beyond agree that we grew up in the "best of times and in the most wonderful country ever." I was raised in Odessa as an only child, and I remember the day when doors to our houses could be left unlocked, when as a ten-year-old, I could ride my bike across town to see my grand folks, and a time when your word and a handshake sealed the deal. My, how times have changed … sad, isn't it? I recall the song by The Judds ("Grandpa Tell Me About the Good Ol' Days") that was played on guitar and sung by my son at my dad's memorial service some seventeen years ago. That's where *I* am right now. It's sobering.

And with all the political, cultural, and racial divide in our nation now, I can't help but wonder where we're headed. The anger, the vitriol, and the hostility toward those who disagree with a particular narrative is especially alarming. Then it comes to me — who's *really* in control here? … *Is anyone?* The Good Book says God is. Our Maker, our Creator. He knows all this stuff going on. He's omniscient *and* omnipotent. I mean, right at the time I was writing the first draft of this story, there was a little one just-a-growin' in my daughter's body. He or she was about the size of a perfectly shaped lime, and the gender had already been determined. This yet unborn, unseen child even had a detectable heartbeat racing about 150 beats per minute (twice the speed of mother Noelle.)

You know what that is? It's a miracle … not just some evolving mesh of flesh, bone, and tissue that somehow fuses together and in thirty-nine weeks, suddenly out comes a baby. I think Jeremiah 1:15 (NIV) says it perfectly: "Before you were formed in the womb I knew you, before you were born, I set you apart." We should all marvel at the thought. This little child is a gift of love from above. It's one way God tells us, "I'm not through with the human race just yet. There is still hope. There is still a reason to live … a reason for life."

Despite all these things going on in our world, I take great comfort in knowing He has a plan. For me, my family, and even this little child whom I already loved and had never even met yet. Knowing in all likelihood, this was to be the last one, I endeavored more than ever to savor and cherish these precious fleeting moments that would be coming our way — from my first sight of this little infant, to the first cry and the first poop. It's all still a miracle … how else could one explain: one second, this little bitty baby gets its oxygen and nutrition from an umbilical cord, and then the next moment he/she is breathing the air we breathe, all on its own? It's a divine act of the Lord God Almighty, and I feel very privileged to be here to experience it.

Yep, it's no secret Carolyn and I were hoping for a little granddaughter, this last grandchild. But regardless, we know that children are a reward from the Lord (Psalm 12:3), and do not and will not take this gift — this child — lightly or for granted. I shall appreciate the first yawn, the first smile, the first giggle all the more. It's my last go around, and I'm going to bask in the Good Lord's goodness to me as never before.

P.S. Okay, here's the deal: the way I liked to figure it, the odds are greatly in our favor for this grandchild (#6) to be a girl — a 96.8% chance — after FIVE grandsons in a row. Go figure. Others say it's really 50 – 50. Whatever. If it is a boy, he must be VERY special. But think of the odds. Statistics don't lie, or so they say. It's just how you choose to look at it. Right?

*On January 31, 2021, at 2:11 p.m., family and friends all celebrated as PINK flares shot forth from the gender reveal powder cannons! (Lilly Grace was born August 17, 2021, to parents Zach and Noelle and to especially proud grandparents Charlie and Carolyn). I still think "Norma" has a nice flair to it.*

## *Written by Grandfather Norman to My Only Granddaughter A Few Hours Before She Was Born*

Gettin' all doodied up for first night out

Today, in about four hours, you, my sweet granddaughter, will be entering into this world. It's your *real* first birthday. What a joyous occasion it will be for all of our family! And being the only *girl* out of five other wonderful grandkids, you're very special. So, get ready to be spoiled! We love you already and haven't even met you yet, Miss Lilly Grace. Well, that is your name as of now, but your mom has told us she just might change it, but won't know for sure until she's seen you.

Matters not — your folks could name you "Sasquatch" and we'd still be in love.

For we all know you, my dear little one, are a gift from God above (Psalm 127:3). Today, our world and country is in chaos. There is much hatred, divisiveness, and violence all around us. For us older folks, we've never seen the likes of the kind of rampant looting, killing, and disrespect for the rule of law that we hear of and see in the media every day. So-called "systemic racism" is pitting Black folks against the White, and the Browns against the Blacks, and so on. On top of that, we're all battling this worldwide pandemic known as COVID-19. Your mom has been extra vigilant to keep from catching this virus, mainly because she wanted you to be safe, sound, and healthy.

But all this stuff is not new to the world. It's been that way throughout world history and will remain that way until Kingdom Come. What's the answer then? The better question is: WHO'S the answer? It's JESUS. Yes, the only perfect man who has ever lived and still lives. I pray, sweet one, that you come to know Him as your Lord and Savior early in your life by receiving Him into your heart (John 1:12). I waited until I was twenty-two-years-old, but I only wish I'd come into that marvelous relationship with Him earlier on. You see, even now in these last few remaining hours in your mommy's womb, God is still forming you ... and He knows exactly what He's doing. He also knows the plans He has for you, plans to give you a future and a hope (Jeremiah 29:11). So, despite all the strife and turmoil that surrounds us now and in the days to come in my life and yours, we have hope. Because as that glorious song bids us to sing: "Because He Lives ... We Can Face Tomorrow ... All Fear Is Gone ... Because I Know He Holds the Future ... Just Because He Lives." You will bring much joy to our lives. And you will have joy in yours — countless beautiful, wonderful times with your family and friends. And when Jesus lives in your heart, you can have *peace* in the midst of the storms of life that will surely come your way. Better than even all that, you'll have the assurance of heaven and life eternal, forever and ever, along with those who've trusted in the Lord Jesus in this broken world. I love you, my sweet and only granddaughter, forever and forever myself… and can hardly wait to make your acquaintance.

See you soon,<br>DaddyO

My quiver is wonderfully full

## 26

# DAPHNE FAY –
# THE WONDER PUG

About three years ago, my wife Carolyn and I got a pug puppy. They don't come any cuter than little pugs. I took Daphne Fay with me to a lot of places early on, especially when she was easy to carry in my arms. Invariably, people (especially the ladies) would stop whatever they were doing to come over and "ooh and aah" over her and want to pet this seven-pound bundle of cuteness. Whether it was at the bank, the drug store, or the YMCA, the reaction was always the

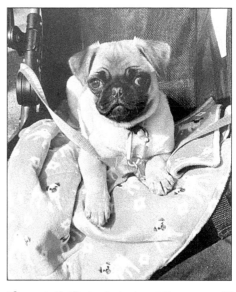

"So cute!" "But what about the puppy?"

same: "Oh, so adorable … How sweet … I want one … Makes my day."

*Now* I know why my son wanted a puppy when in college. Go figure. It even happened to *me* at the Glen Rose soccer park walking track while going out for a little morning exercise. I was clipping right along with little Daphne on a leash when two nice middle-aged ladies (whom I actually know) passed me going in the opposite direction. One of them hollered back to me, "So adorable!" My response: "Well, thank you! ... but what about the puppy?!" Corny, I know, but that's what I do...

Originating in sixteenth century China, the pug has been described as a "big dog in a little package." That's Daphne Fay alright. She thinks our large yard, front and back, is her territory. I mean, when I let her out first thing in the morning to do her business, she takes off a runnin' like a greyhound at the races. Just shoots straight out the backdoor looking to and fro for anything that moves, be it a squirrel, rabbit, bird, or whatever. She's just-a-barking, letting all yard critters and the world know "this here is *my* territory." Carolyn and I call this daily ritual "domaining."

Now Daphne Fay does have her annoying quirks alright. Sometimes she won't come when called. Stubborn ... stubborn. Daphne doesn't close her mouth when she eats and "smacks" a lot, too. She gets into things she ought not to. And periodically, she'll drag up something organic (often times bigger than she is) from out of nowhere and seems very content to ingest whatever "that" was — we don't even want to know. Moreover, almost anything new left on the floor in the house is fair game for her, and she thinks it was brought in for her enjoyment. She has a shoe fetish, too. Not good. You can ask Carolyn about that one. But she is great with our grandkids. That's her saving grace with the wife. "Daph" thinks the kids have come just to see her when they're over at the house, and she dutifully follows them along on little hiking trails around our property when they're visiting. She never snaps at them and actually likes it when they pull her tail.

Daphne also loves to do "zoomies" around the kids, just to let 'em know she's happy they're there. Many a time we find her waiting patiently in the hallway seated at the closed bedroom door, awaiting a sleeping little boy to arise from his nap. She's smart, too. At night when it's time for bed, it's the strangest thing — all I have to do is say: "Beddy-bye time" and off she goes, dashing cheerfully and obediently into her sleeping pen. Some dog, that Daph.

In all my years I've never seen a dog watch television the way Daphne Fay does. I mean, she really watches it and reacts to it, too. She'll even huff, puff, and bark and stand on her hind legs if she spots another dog (or animal) on the screen, like she could really do something ... yeah, right. She barks at these animals she sees on the screen (acting *so* tough). The thing is, most of these animals in real life could, well ... let's just say, easily devour her as an appetizer.

But it seems Daph's favorite shows are the old-time Westerns. She especially likes *Bonanza* ... and *particularly* Little Joe. Occasionally I've even caught Daphne sitting front and center in the living room just staring at Little Joe when I'd be passing through the room. Problem is, one time I discovered she wasn't alone. Wife Carolyn was sittin' there doing the very same thing. We gotta have a talk.

## 27

# ONE FINE FELLOW — TRUE LOVE WAYS

Though Gary Thompson and I attended Austin Elementary and Crockett Junior High together in the early '60s (he was one grade behind me), I didn't really know Gary until my junior year at Odessa High. Should have. We had so much in common — no siblings, both sets of parents graduated from OHS in the early '40s, we took our education pretty seriously, and we were selected "Most Dependable" by our classmates. We were both church goers and pretty much lived our lives in the straight and narrow. Not to say we didn't occasionally have a little innocent, mischievous fun, mind you. We did.

We worked on the school newspaper together where I wrote feature articles, and Gary covered sports. I was involved in Student Council, and good ol' Gary played the trumpet in the school band (always seated as first or second chair.) He wasn't flashy or pretentious. He was just a really quality, humble guy who was jovial, smart, and a friend to everybody who knew him. Everybody loved Gary. No wonder he was elected President of the OHS Student Body his senior year.

He possessed a corny kind of laugh that was just infectious … and I've been infected ever since. To this day, I mimic this sort of happy, nonsensical utterance whenever he used to play with his pet dachshund "Shotsy." By habit I guess, one can hear me, "Eh … heh, heh, heh, heh" whenever I'm playing with my little pug. That became a part of *my* lexicon decades ago. I got that from Gary.

But it was *my* senior year that we got to be pretty close. We were lab partners in Mr. Gunn's chemistry class. We got along great — that is until he ended up charring my "unknown" (he claimed *"inadvertently"*) by being a little overzealous with our shared Bunsen burner. The thing was, I was almost finished with this two-day process of identifying my random substance for the final exam portion of the class. That's when I smelled something smoking and looked over to see *my* "unknown" cooking like a charcoaled crispy critter. I had to start all over! Was I happy amateur chemist-not-to-be? Nope. Was that revenge on Gary's part for the broken nose he got playing/losing against my team for the school championship in intramural flag football? Nope. I knew that, because Gary has no mean streak in his being.

Once, Gary came over to my house to spend the night while my folks were out of town for a weekend trip. We decided to make pancakes for breakfast the next morning — without eggs in the mix (my idea). Not good. Let's just say our experience as chemistry lab partners didn't help us one iota. Those pancakes tasted like stale cardboard. Not good.

Little did I know when I went off to Texas Tech after graduation, I had planted a seed in Gary's mind that he might just want to do the same thing. He hadn't particularly been thinking of going off to college much until he drove up to Lubbock to

Gary and me at Texas Tech

visit me up at Tech one weekend. He thought, "You know, I can do this. I should do this." So, he did, and joined me in the dorm at Carpenter Hall on campus that next fall. He also joined my fraternity, and we "was brothers." I introduced him to my good buddy and roommate Gordon, and they hit it off well and are good buds to this day.

By the time Gary graduated from Tech with a degree in mathematics, he had married his high school sweetheart, Carol Scott, who'd also come up to Lubbock go to school at Tech. Of all the couples I have known over the decades who married early on in life, I'd have to say that Gary and Carol Scott were truly the perfect match. I believe they were made for each other. Gary went to work for Phillips Petroleum in Odessa, Bartlesville, Oklahoma, and then Borger, Texas, before retiring from the company after twenty-eight years. The couple had two boys (Matt and Greg) along the way. After Phillips, Gary then taught 9th grade algebra for four years at Borger High. It was then that Southern Union Oil Company in Midland lured him back to the Permian Basin (Midland-Odessa area) the summer of 2006, because the company knew of Gary's knowledge and experience in the gas industry.

The Thompsons bought a nice house in Midland, found a good church home, and were getting all adjusted, when Gary went off to work in downtown Midland as usual the morning of February 28, 2008. Shortly after arriving at the office, Gary felt a sharp pain in his chest and collapsed to the floor in the coffee breakroom. With no warning signs, he had experienced what's known a "massive ascending aorta aneurysm." It came on so quickly and out of nowhere. Only a very small percentage of people survive the magnitude of such a trauma. Midland ER doctors said about his only chance of making it was to somehow get him to M.D. Anderson in Houston by care flight and be treated by specialists there. Precious time was of the essence. But it was gonna take a miracle for him to survive a flight, if they could even get one. God gave him that miracle. A private jet flew him (and Carol) the ninety-minute flight to Houston where emergency surgery was performed by the doctors who were prepared and awaiting his arrival. They told Carol to prepare herself for his death. They gave him about a 1% chance of making it through the night. But after sixteen hours of surgery (and multiple strokes in the midst of it all), Gary pulled through — because he's a fighter, and the Good Lord still had plans for Gary.

But one must know Gary was not the Gary we were all used to. He was something akin to "infant" state — no walking, no talking, NO memory... No feeding himself, no recognizing family, no nothing. He remained in intensive care a month at St. Luke's hospital and then was sent on to an acute care hospital for another month with minimal chance of recovery. It was suggested to Carol that the family consider putting him in a nursing home in Midland. Not this guy. At the last minute, Carol found out there might possibly be another option there in Houston ... a rehab facility (TIRR) that has had some success with such patients. "We'll go there." He required con-stant care, specialized nurses, and intense and challenging therapies ... and six

surgeries over a three-year period. There were setbacks too — like a *DESCENDING* aorta, prostate cancer, loss of his voice, aphasia, and apraxia, you name it ... Gary had it, and is still a survivor. Fifteen years now of two slow steps forward, and one step backwards. It's the new normal for my friend and his family all this time.

When in Midland on occa-sion, I get to visit Gary and Carol. I stand in awe of how the Good Lord allowed doctors to repair a physically broken heart so that the

True love lived out

inner heart of one courageous, kind soul, could be a witness and reminder to us all of God's grace. Gary's not bitter but grateful. There's no self-pity in this man, only an appreciation of each day he's given … they're given. His wife, his two sons (and wives), and three granddaughters are the benefactors and testament of God's bigger plan for each of them … and you and me. But, you know, Carol is also the heroine in all this. She said to me last time I visited, as I was leaving, "I sure love that guy." After fifty years of marriage, Gary and Carol still live out the lyrics of a song composed some sixty-five years ago by Lubbock's own favorite son, Buddy Holly — "True Love Ways." If you are privileged to know the Thompsons, you know what I mean.

## 28

# GENTLE TEACHER'S GESTURE
# TURNED ME AROUND

Each May, when National Teacher's Day rolls around, I think back on many of the teachers that had a positive influence in my life. And there were many. One of the first that comes to mind was Mr. Lewis Roberson, my 7th grade "Advanced Math" class teacher. Mr. Roberson was probably in his late fifties, balding, of small stature, wore glasses, and the first male teacher I ever had. I was intimidated by him and the subject he'd be teaching (Advanced

One Gentle Man

Math) from the get-go. Now I was pretty smart, but the first time I walked into his class and looked around, I could just tell there were some really smart dudes and dudettes in there ... Jesse, Janeen, and Jimmy, just to name a few.

Mr. Roberson started calling roll alphabetically by last name. Even that was intimidating. I was used to hearing an upbeat, personable "Charlie" from a sweet woman's voice instead of the monotone, impersonal "Norman" I got from Mr. Roberson. He passed out our yellow soft-cover "Advanced Mathematics" text books; and as I skimmed through it, I got this sick kind of feeling inside. There were graphs and diagrams and symbols in there I'd never seen before. I thought, "Oh boy, what have I got myself into?" Mr. Roberson assigned us the first two problems in the book for homework for the next day's class. "Brain Teasers" were what they were called. Things like, "An athlete is able to jump forever, but each time he jumps, he gets a little more tired. Every jump goes 1/2 as far as the previous jump. On the very first jump, he goes one foot. The next jump he goes only 1/2 foot and so on. The question is, how many jumps does it take him to go two feet?" The answer — He NEVER gets to the two-foot mark because you keep adding smaller and smaller amounts.

Well, my twelve-year-old brain wasn't used to thinking like this. Still isn't. For me, these weren't "brain teasers." They were "brain hurts." I did not get the answer(s). Jesse did. He got 'em all … from then on, too. (Six years later, Jesse got a full scholarship to the academically-elite Rice University for six years … what does that tell you?). I was distraught. I thought everybody else got the answers. I did not know they were just like me. This went on for about a week, and my parents could tell I was unhappy. I told them about math class and Mr. Roberson and how I was *not* getting it.

What's a parent to do? My dad called Mr. Roberson on the phone, and I heard them talking. I don't know what my daddy said exactly, but I was a little embarrassed and relieved at the same time. Next day in math class, right after roll call, Mr. Roberson said, "Norman, come with me a minute." We stepped out into the hall and walked down toward the water fountain and, in essence, this is what he said to me in a soft, gentle, reassuring voice: "Charlie, your dad called last night. We had a nice conversation. Listen, son, you're going to do just fine in this class. These math problems this first week or so are just to get you and your classmates to thinking in a way you might not have done before. To stretch you a bit. Truth be known, most of your fellow students aren't getting the answers either. Jesse does, but he's the exception. He's actually exceptional. Now *YOU* are a smart kid or you wouldn't have been placed in this class. Next week we'll be getting into a different type of math. You study hard, ask questions, and try the best you can, and *you will get this*. I'll help you, and I'll be your friend. Besides all that, you're a Norman, and I know your granddaddy, Charles Sr. You got good genes, Charles III."

That two-minute conversation in the hallway of Crockett Junior High School in the fall of 1962 changed my thinking about male teachers, my confidence level in academia, thoughts toward my peers/friends, and those in authority. From then on, at least once a week, when Mr. Roberson called roll and came to my name, instead of saying the usual monotone "Norman," without looking up, he'd call out "#3." It was his way of acknowledging me as an individual and not just some random kid in his class. Made me feel special... little things.

I learned lots of things in Mr. Roberson's class. We learned how to fill out tax returns (Forms 990, 1040, etc.), and we even got our Social Security cards through his class. We also learned why, "when all else fails," follow instructions. For instance, one day we had a three-page exam. A "pop quiz" ... oh, how I hated those! He told us we had a maximum of thirty minutes to complete it and when finished, to put it up on his desk. The very first sentence read in all caps: *BEFORE COMPLETING THIS EXAM READ ALL QUESTIONS/ INSTRUCTIONS FIRST.* Like everybody else it seemed, I glanced over it pretty quickly and just started filling in the answers to the questions. The problems were not that difficult, and I finished the test in short order. Then, right at the end, after the last problem, I noticed a sentence at the bottom that made me kinda sick... again. It read in regular type: "Now that you have come to the end of the exam, do NOT answer any of the problems (leave them blank), simply sign your name in the space provided, and bring your paper to the front desk. You get an "A" on the exam if you followed instructions." No wonder Jesse handed his paper in about two minutes into the test. I thought he was just being Jesse again. He was, and got his usual "A."

ALL of this is to say to you teachers out there on the front line, those of you with our kids and grandkids every day, *YOU ARE APPRECIATED!* It's a much different, more difficult world than the one I faced growing up. I can hardly imagine. But *you* can be a force for good. You never know what an encouraging word, a warm and kind smile, or a heartfelt pep talk to a discouraged young person might do to change a life. *THANK YOU* for what you do! Who knows? Maybe some sixty years from now someone might write a story about you.

# 29

# RESPECT FOR A MAN OF HONOR (PART II)

A few years ago, I had the honor to meet, know, and write about a very special individual — ninety-five-year-old (at the time) WWII veteran Hewitt Gomez of Lafayette, Louisiana. Hewitt served in the Army Air Corps in the war as a secret agent and flight navigator of an elite squadron of men whose mission was to fly highly classified "Special Operations" to deliver arms, supplies, and specially trained agents into Nazi-occupied Europe in late 1943 – May 1945. They were collectively known by the codename "The Carpetbaggers." I wrote about Hewitt's experiences and heroics (of which he humbly deflected to his fellow servicemen) in my book *Remembrances* (Jan-Carol Publishing 2021) — a compilation of thirty-two short stories published in the *Glen Rose Reporter* newspaper from 2018 – 2020.

Well, the thing is, I sent a copy of *Remembrances* last summer to a former roommate of mine from way back named David, and his wife Stephanie, who live outside Opelika, Alabama. It wasn't long after that I got the call. Stephanie told me she almost fell out of her chair when she came across the story I had written about Hewitt. She *knows* Hewitt personally ... and told me *her father was also one of the very few remaining survivors* of The Carpetbaggers — 103 years-young Mr. Orrin "Boody" Brown Jr. Stephanie had gotten to know Hewitt personally through reunions and various gatherings of the Carpetbaggers by accompanying her father to related functions over the many years.

Out of the hundreds of men who flew some 3,000 night-time sorties (Fall of 1943 – Spring 1945), now there's only a handful still with us ... and I knew I just couldn't let this opportunity pass me by. If he agreed and was up to it, I'd love to meet Mr. Brown – to learn of his life experiences and then tell some of *his* story, too. So, Stephanie arranged it all, and I flew to Alabama and was privileged to spend a couple hours on a recent Sunday afternoon with Stephanie and her father. "Boody" is quite the character – a man of faith, he's an humble, quick-witted, feisty, patriotic centenarian who loves our country dearly. Born an only child on April 4, 1920, in Opelika, he grew up in the area and attended Alabama Polytechnical Institute before the school later became known as Auburn University. He studied aeronautical administration, graduating there in the summer of 1941 – a few months prior to Pearl Harbor and the United States' entry into WWII.

He decided he wanted to join the Army Air Corp as an Aviation Cadet, but it seems there was a problem. You see, Boody was (and still is) of a particular small physical stature. When he went down to the local Armed Services Recruitment Center to enlist, his height at 5'5" barely met the criteria alright ... but, well, his weight of 108 pounds *was* an issue. He missed the minimum requirement by two pounds – 110 was the cutoff. Realizing that Orrin Brown was really a top-notch prospect, the recruiter told him he could have one more chance at weigh-in the next day and gave him a suggestion: "Come back tomorrow; and just before you get here, eat as many *bananas* and drink as much water as you can, and we'll see where you stand." He did just that and came in at a bloated 112 pounds ... and couldn't stomach the thought of eating bananas for quite some time thereafter! But, hey, a man's gotta do what a man's gotta do.

So, Orrin was sworn in as an official Aviation Cadet in January, 1942; then it was off for training as a Bombardier Navigator at the Army Air base in Victorville, California. Upon successful completion of the courses/training there, he was assigned to "anti-submarine patrol" at the Marine Corps Air Station located in Cherry Point, North Carolina. His duty as part of an eight-man crew flying "antiquated" Lockheed 829s was to scout and patrol the shores of the mid-Atlantic states looking for German U-boats known to have been lurking along the Eastern seaboard during this time. His job as Bombardier Navigator was to peer through the front clear-glass

Bombardier Navigator
Orrin "Boody" Brown

nose of the aircraft, recognize the target, and open the Bombay Doors at just the right time for the bombs/payload to be released. Of course, assuming it was the *right* target. Orrin recalls the time early in his patrolling days when he mistook a *blue whale* for an enemy submarine that sent the crew scrambling for a potential drop. Fortunately for the whale, Orrin realized his mistake just in time to abort the release of the depth charges. But it was an invaluable experience for the young navigator and for the bigger job that lay ahead a few months down the road.

In the summer of 1943, Orrin and his squadron were ordered to England where, after a few months, they were assigned to serve alongside the Royal Air Force in anti-submarine duty. A short time later Orrin was selected to become a part of an elite, secretive specially-trained group of airmen with the extremely dangerous mission of flying night-time sorties to assist various "Resistance Fighters" throughout occupied Europe. They flew modified B-24 "Ds" aircraft that were painted all-black (to minimize detection at night) and reconfigured to meet the needs of delivering weapons, munitions, food, supplies, and secret agent resistance-fighters to aid those battling the Germans in their own homeland. "The Carpetbagger Project" involved more than 3,000 sorties, dropped over 20,000 containers/11,000 packages of vital supplies (including twenty-six messenger pigeons); 7,000 tons of operational equipment; and over 1,000 parachutists from the Fall of 1943 – Spring of 1945. The Carpetbaggers were stationed out of Harrington Air Field, England's clandestine military base some eighty miles northwest of London. They flew extremely low to the ground (400 feet for supplies/600 feet for parachutists) with speeds ranging from 200 – 300 m.p.h. for their drops to resistance groups in France, Holland, Belgium, Denmark, Norway, and Yugoslavia. There were over 350,000 resistance members who were aided by these covert efforts on behalf of the Allies the last eighteen months of the war.

Orrin and his crew of eight carried out some thirty missions that usually lasted several tension-filled hours. Eighteen of his flights were over France. Things were so secretive that only the pilot, the navigator, and the bombardier knew the destination/location of where the drop was supposed to be, and *they* only found that out about an hour or two from High Command shortly before departure. They did not even know what cargo they would be carrying — as the plane would taxi out for a takeoff position and wait for notification from the tower that their plane had been loaded from underneath/behind and was cleared for departure. Needless to say, in every flight there was always the lingering thought they might never make it back safely to England, or home to the USA for that matter ... fighting for the freedom they themselves may never experience again. One time in particular, Orrin remembers a flight over Norway where his crew experienced a significant amount of flak from German anti-aircraft guns. They were the second of two Carpetbagger planes flying about a mile behind the lead plane when all of a sudden it seemed like a barrage of fireworks exploded all around them. What seemed like a lifetime was only a few brief moments until they were out of sight and range of enemy fire. Though sustaining some noticeable damage, the plane was able to make it back to Harrington to be repaired to fight another day. Providence ruled the day.

Over the decades, Orrin, Hewitt, and other Carpetbagger survivors have had numerous reunions and various recognition ceremonies. I asked Orrin if there was one in particular that stood out. Without hesitation he recalled a phone call he received about 3:00 a.m. in late 1999. It was from a Mr. Marc Verschooris, a young Belgian man with a strong European accent asking to speak with "Mr. Orrin Brown." This man explained he was a high school math teacher and was writing a book about a local WWII hero and the Belgium resistance near his city of Ghent, Belgium. He knew there had been a Carpetbagger drop that took place in a rural area near the town in 1944; and through extensive research, he was able to track down which plane and crew had made the run. Orrin Brown was indeed the Navigator Bombardier for that flight. Mr. Verschooris invited Orrin to come to Ghent as an honored guest for an official Ceremony and Reception to be given in honor of those

who helped his fellow countrymen in the Resistance. Orrin did go and was awarded The Belgian Cross at a ceremony at the Ghent Town Hall in June 2000, commemorating the valor and sacrifice of those who fought alongside the Belgians in their quest for freedom from Nazi occupation. Orrin was especially humbled and appreciative that even after fifty years the Belgian people still have not forgotten the willingness to fight alongside them by him and his fellow American soldiers to free the Belgium from the Nazis.

Those involved with The Carpetbagger Project were sworn to secrecy for fifty years. Even spouses/family members after the war were forbidden to be told *anything* about The Carpetbaggers' missions and purposes. Severe punishment awaited anyone who broke the code/oath. That's why it was only in the late 1990s that the public began to find out about these secret war heroes. Orrin is the last surviving member of his squadron and was recognized/honored at Auburn's 2022 season opening football game against Mercer as Auburn's oldest living ROTC alumnae. As I talked with him about that and these other accolades, I sensed a bit of humility and self-deprecation in his person. I told Mr. Brown in front of his daughter Stephanie how much my generation appreciates his sacrifice and willingness to serve and give, so that we and millions of others can live ... in freedom. And that I will teach and remind my grandchildren what he and his fellow countryman did so that we could grow up in the most wonderful country (despite its flaws) ever in the history of the world. In a strange kinda way, I think he felt a little undeserving of all this attention, notoriety, and accolades. Like so many of his time, it seems they felt they were just doing their job, that they did what was right, and that they did it well. And somehow, *they* survived when so many others did not. It was an especially poignant moment in my time with Mr. Orrin "Boody" Brown Jr. — and not uncharacteristic of his, "The Greatest Generation."

Honored to meet another veteran of
"The Greatest Generation"

*Addendum: What follows is an entry I wrote in 2002 in Part Eight of "A Journal of Personal Reactions" in the book "Now You Know ... Reactions after seeing the movie Saving Private Ryan." What I wrote some twenty years ago is as applicable today as it was in 2002 and in 1945 at the end of WWII:}*

"*Of all the movies I have seen in my life,* SAVING PRIVATE RYAN *stands among the top. I'll never forget it. Just as the veterans of WWII (or any war, for that matter) will always remember the horrors, fears, cruelty, and sacrifices of combat, I'll remember this movie. I guess because the older I get (fifty-two-years-old as I wrote this), the more I cherish my country, my parents, my heritage, and my life. Traveling as I do and reading what I read, I know the freedom we experience in the United States is not free and came with a great price.*

*My dad is old now, a veteran of the Pacific War. After seeing the movie, in which tears flowed freely (especially the first thirty minutes, but throughout as well), I wrote an open letter of appreciation addressed to all US Military veterans. I sent copies to my dad and my father-in-law expressing my deep gratitude and thanksgiving for their sacrifice. If I'd been born thirty years earlier, that could have been me rushing the shores of Normandy or Iwo Jima. I wondered how I would have felt. Or come out.*

*I guess as a way of honoring these brave men who gave the supreme sacrifice (or were willing to do so), I take it upon myself to personally thank them whenever I have the chance. I had my son (fourteen-years-old at the time) read about D-Day and do a short report before seeing this movie, his first R-rated show. I even took my whole family to France in July 2000 to walk the shoreline of Normandy Beach where our way of life and freedom from tyranny for millions of people hung in the balance those first few days in June 1944.*

SAVING PRIVATE RYAN *obviously touched a nerve with me. I was proud, deeply saddened, extremely moved. As one young German said after seeing the movie in his own country, 'That was not an anti-German movie, it was an anti-war movie.' God Bless all of our veterans and* GOD BLESS AMERICA.*"*

# 30

# AWKWARD MOMENTS JUST A PART OF GROWING UP

You've got 'em. I've got 'em. All God's chillens got 'em ... those awkward moments in time we can laugh at now, but at the time, well... you know.

So, it was with me, way back in 1964 at Crockett Junior High School in Odessa. I was in the 8th grade and taking art class as an elective. It's good to know that I always liked the girls and was pretty popular I guess, but I was very self-conscious about having braces on my teeth. For two years, I endured the name-calling — "Metal Mouth, Brace Face, etc.," while my teeth were being straightened. It was toward the end of the school year when I finally got my braces off and got to smile again! That next day in class, the art teacher, Miss Lorette, volunteered me to be the "model" for a portrait drawing session. I happily agreed and took my place on a chair on a table for my fellow students to do a pencil sketch. I noticed that the girls seemed especially attentive, and may I say, "cheerful." They were grinning big-time, whispering among themselves; and I, for the first time in two years, did smile back unabashedly. I just knew they were admiring my new pearly whites and noticing my straight teeth. Maybe so, but the main thing they noticed — my fly was open! Forty-five long minutes' worth! Class bell rang, I hopped down, and was so proud of myself. That is, until my pal Alan walked by, and told me I ought to check out my zipper before I got too smug. *Oh my gosh!* … I was so embarrassed. I can't believe it! No wonder the girls were snickering and smiling so cute-like! Am I over it? Pretty much … fifty-five years later, the memory still lingers though. Whatever.

Fast forward a few years, and I'm taking trigonometry in high school. Now I was pretty smart and studied hard, but there were others in my class that were smarter — they just had it. You know the type. Like Barney Fife used to say, "Some people want it and can't get it. I got it and can't get rid of it." Well, that was *NOT* me … that was Jesse, Clay, Bruce, Janeen … those types. Anyway, one day in Trig class, ol' Mr. Kuser asked who got the *right* answer on a particular homework assignment. He'd already told us the correct answer. Well, I'm thinking, it's probably better to raise your hand that you "got it right" than not raise your hand at all. So, I half-way raised my hand and sure enough, Mr. Kuser called on me, "Norman, you got that answer? Put it on the board and explain how you got it." (You need to know, for many students — the smartest ones — they loved Mr. Kuser … I was in that other category who was intimidated by him). So, I diffidently got up in front of the class and started putting the problem on the board. About halfway through, Mr. Kuser interrupted me and said, "Norman, see that negative there, isn't that supposed to be a positive?" I started trying to figure that out. "No, sir. It won't work if I change it." "Go ahead then." So, I kept on-a-going. He questioned me a second time. I kept on going. Finally, I came to the end, explaining to everyone how I had come up with the answer. Mr. Kuser told me to have a seat. I was so relieved; I think I might have even slightly "relieved myself" in the process. Then Mr. Kuser said something to the class like this: "Norman got the right answer alright. But not correctly. He actually came up with a 'double negative' that produced the right answer the wrong way." Do not do that. I learned the hard way how the expression "two wrongs don't make a right" can apply to math problems, too.

Okay, last one. My school was the Odessa High Bronchos... cross-town rivals to the uppity better-known school, the Odessa Permian Panthers. Though I would have liked to have played varsity sports, I was of slight stature and just not big enough. But I still loved the games, and football was my favorite. As a senior, somehow, I was selected to be the *one* guy in school to be the judge/monitor of how intense and loud the "spirit" was at our pep rallies in cheering for our team. The shop class had built a large fifteen foot wooden "horse-

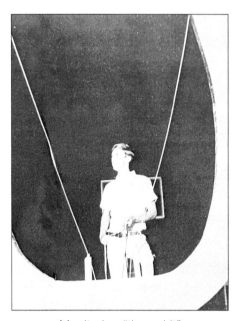

Monitoring "the spirit" before the big rip

shoe" (remember our mascot was a "Broncho") placed flat on a platform with a hinge, pulley, and ropes — this horseshoe could be "raised" vertically 90 degrees by pulling on the ropes. So, the idea was this contraption was to be an indicator of sorts for how loud the student body cheered for the team. The louder, the more erect the horseshoe. I would pull on the ropes and sometimes it would hover at 45 – 60 – 75 degrees, then finally be straight up perpendicular (90 degrees) if the noise level was really loud. It was my call. Anyway, the last game/pep rally was for Permian. I was getting all situated in center court of the field house as the student body of 1,500 started filling the bleachers. The cheerleaders were a few feet right behind me, and the football team and coaches were lined up right behind them. I went over to check the knots on the pulley one more time, bent over, and "RIP!" Uh oh ... my pants had just ripped in the back all the way... can I say it? Down the crack! I'm in a mell of a hess. I can't leave. I'm stuck. What to do!? The rally was due to start in one minute, and all eyes were on me! So, in a panic, I untucked my favorite blue Ban-Lon shirt and pulled that thing as far down in back as it could go. I pulled and pulled (trying to be as discreet as one can be with 3,000 eyes peering down). It stretched just below the cheeks ... that is, if I "hunkered up" just so and didn't move. The rally started, and I was just hoping *nobody* — especially the pretty cheerleaders right behind me — would notice my behind. For some twenty minutes I was stiff-shouldered slouching backwards. I gave new meaning to "tucking one's tail" as I high-tailed it on home right after the rally to change pants. Never did wear that Ban-Lon again either. Am I embarrassed by any of these things anymore? Nope. As a seventy-three-year-old, I'm over it and mighty proud of it actually.

# 31

# BROTHERS IN MORE
# WAYS THAN ONE

A couple of months ago I received the fall/winter 2023 issue of *The Shield of Phi Kappa Psi*, my college fraternity's biannual magazine. Though I've not really been involved in fraternity activities since my days at Texas Beta (Texas Tech 1969 – 1972), I like to browse through the pages and catch up on the Chapter and affairs of the national organization, as well as read of those who've received awards or passed on to Chapter Eternal, etc. – all with fond remembrances of those good times and friends back in the day.

Being somewhat of a sentimentalist, lately I've been thinking back on many people in my past who've had a positive impact in my life. Among my good fraternity brothers, there was one guy in particular that kept coming to mind. He'd actually been a significant influence on me, and he didn't even know it. I wondered if I could somehow find this brother and tell him of such (if he's even still around). So, when I saw the phone number listed for Phi Kappa Psi HQ in the magazine, I called, and Kathy answered. I told her I'd sure like to try to contact "Brant McGlothlin," a fraternity brother at Texas Beta whom I only knew for about a year in 1969 – 70 (a senior when I was a sophomore). Friendly as she was, she put me on hold, and a couple minutes later came up with "Captain William Brant McGlothlin," two old phone numbers, and the last address they had on file (Rockport, Texas). I bet that's him! Sure enough, the numbers were out of service, so I decided to write this guy a short greeting card — asking for a response (if it got to him), and if he happened to be the Brant I knew from some fifty-three years ago back in Lubbock? Two weeks later I heard back. Yes indeed!

You see, back in 1970 or so, Brother Brant shared with our fraternity brothers at a Phi Psi meeting how he had become a true *Christ-follower*... basically, he just told us his faith story. I listened from afar, and though not particularly interested at the time, I never forgot his boldness and the courage it must have taken to stand up and tell others of his new-found faith. I admired that and thought he was a good example of someone that I might aspire to be like someday. Not at that time, mind you — too many other worldly distractions (dorm job, intramural sports, coeds/new friends, trying to figure out a major/career path, fraternity, etc.). So that was that... but deep down, I knew Brant had *something* I did not have.

Come to find out, we had quite a bit more in common than I realized. Growing up in west Texas, we both loved sports (football especially), were good students, and good ol' church-goers from our youths — but in the latter teenage years, we both pretty much dropped out of the church scene and became somewhat uninterested in spiritual things (to the point of agnosticism for Brant). But Brant had met a gal his junior year at Tech that he was really interested in, who invited him to join her at a Campus Crusade for Christ (CCC, now CRU) meeting. He went (just to be with her), and it was quite an awakening for Brant, who at the time was searching for purpose and direction in his own life. There he witnessed fellow students who had *this something* ... a peace, purpose, and direction lacking in his own life. He heard the life-transforming message of the Gospel of Jesus Christ there. A couple of days later, one of the guys from the CRU team came by and shared with Brant a small tract known as "The Four Spiritual Laws" — a short, straightforward presentation of the Good News. Later that week, alone at night in his bedroom, Brant made the life-changing, prayerful decision to follow Christ, and his life has never been the same since.

For me, I continued on my merry way through graduation at Tech and then on to graduate school at the University of Texas at Austin. Yet in my heart of hearts, I knew there was something definitely missing in my own life. Though I thought I was a "good guy" alright, I had no real direction, no purpose of what I wanted to do or be. Around this time, I came across this quote (from renowned 17th century French philosopher Blaise Pascal) that spoke to me and my status in life: *"There is a God-shaped vacuum in the heart of every man which cannot be filled by any created thing, but only by the Creator made known in the person of Jesus Christ."*

Hmm ... Shortly after beginning school at UT in the fall of 1972, I was invited to dinner by a distant cousin and her husband (same age and newly-weds); and when we met, I could tell there was something different, something special about them. They, too, were *one of those*. Jim shared with me the same little yellow booklet "The Four Spiritual Laws," and I felt convicted, vulnerable, and humbled. I was thinking *this is what I need.* Then I reflected back on a few people I admired and respected: an outspoken Christian professor at Texas Tech, a gal named Laurie I'd known since my freshman year at Tech who'd turned *her* life around, a couple of guys from my high school in Odessa who'd answered the calling to preach, and even ol' Phi Psi Brother Brant McGlothlin ... was God trying to get my attention?? Like Brant, it took a little while, but all alone one night in my Austin, Texas, apartment bedroom, I prayed the prayer that had the angels in heaven rejoicing. A life changer for me, too.

I went on to finish my graduate degree at UT by 1974, worked in advertising in Hawaii for about three years, and then took a job with a major airline for thirty-four years before retiring in 2010. I'm active in church, do volunteer work, and write short stories for publication. Brant graduated at Tech in January 1971, promptly married Laura (the young lady who invited him to the CRU meeting), and joined pilot training for the United States Air

Force in February and military staff of Campus Crusade. He continued on in ministry work through 1991 during his twenty years of service as a pilot with the USAF. Later, Brant went on to use his education, skills, and experiences to be a Pastor, Administrator, overseas Missionary, Teacher, House Parent in Germany, and a Member Care Coordinator in various ministries in which he continues to this day.

So, Brant and I reconnected after fifty-three years. Never talked on the phone with each other before April 2023. It was akin to talking to a long-lost brother. A Providential connection one might say — *Brothers in fraternity and Brothers in the faith.* Something special indeed!

Fraternity brothers (Brant and Charlie, circa 1970)

Faith brothers (Brant and Charlie, circa 2023)

Brant McGlothlin: wbmcglothlin@gmail.com • Charlie Norman: chas350@outlook.com

# 32

# PEACE OFFICER ON
# THE POLICE FORCE

Though I spent the first eighteen years of my life growing up in Odessa, Texas (in the '50s and '60s), I knew no people of color personally. I had no particular reason to go over across the railroad tracks to the southside where the Black folks lived. So, some fifty years later, when I met Tommey Morris in the spring of 2021, he was the first Black man I'd ever met who still lives my old hometown. I was in town doing research for my book *Road to Reconciliation ... And Beyond (2022)* about the nationally known early '60s "Doo-Wop" singing group, The Velvets, who had its beginnings there. If you want to know about the southside, the Black community from across the tracks, Tommey's your guy ... a gentle, strong, and peaceful man who became a police officer in Odessa, where he served for some thirty years.

Tommey is seventy-nine years-old now and feeling his age. Got arthritis, diabetes, cancer, and A Fib heart condition. But the great thing I've learned about Tommey is he's also got a servant's heart, a giving heart, a forgiving heart ... instilled in him by his mother, his church family, and his school teachers – especially Miss Frizella Whitiker, his English teacher at Blackshear Junior/Senior High School. You see, Tommey grew up in that segregated, discriminatory Jim Crow era of the '50s and early '60s, when the Blacks and

Whites went to different schools, played on separate teams, and did not mix easily or readily with those of a different hue of skin.

But Tommey was different. So was his White friend Don. I was introduced to Tommey through Don, who now lives outside Oklahoma City. Don also grew up on the southside, just a few blocks west of the Black community. They played sports together during the summers (mainly pick-up baseball games) when there were no organized teams as such. They became best friends and hung together regardless. If they happened to go for a hamburger or lunch across the tracks somewhere and the eatery would not allow Tommey to sit with the White patrons, Don would turn away; and they'd find a place that would welcome them both. True friends, those two. But when school started up again, Don went down the street to Ector High School and Tommey to Blackshear. No integration, no mixing allowed.

When I met Tommey, he easily became my friend as well and later even my confidant. He was quite the athlete, too — arguably the best player in football and basketball in his school years at Blackshear. In basketball, he was known as Tommey "The Twister" because of his unique way and talent of slithering around an opponent and making the shot. Just a natural, all-around ball player, that Tommey. So much so that Don wondered if Tommey might could transfer over to Ector to play ball on his teams. It would give Ector's teams a boost in overall athleticism and allow Tommey to be seen by any college coach who might be scouting the area for top-notch athletes. You see, college scouts rarely attended the all-Black league

Tommey "The Twister" –
doing his thing!

games in which Blackshear competed. Don told me that Tommey was so good (and everyone knew), he surely would have been recruited to play college ball if he could only be seen. Around 1960, Don, Tommey, and one of his teachers (and advocate) actually sought out a meeting with the Blackshear principal to seek permission for Tommey to play at Ector to enhance his opportunity for exposure. Unfortunately, the principal informed them that it was not possible and was out of his hands. It was the school district's strict regulations at the time that Black students attend Blackshear only, no exceptions.

Still, Tommey was growing up to be an easy-going, honest, humble, caring man. His mom had taught him well, and Miss Whitiker took a special liking to this kind soul. Mentoring him as only a teacher can, she saw great potential in this soft-spoken young man. Tommey joined the U.S. Air Force upon graduation from Blackshear High and became a Military Police officer (MP) for four years, stationed at Bergstrom Air Force Base in Austin, Texas. Upon completion of his duty there, he returned to Odessa and was hired by the city of Odessa as the fourth Black peace officer in the city's history. As would be expected, there were numerous growing pains that Tommey endured his first years on the force, but Odessa could not have found a better man to exemplify what a true servant of the people should be. He knew the town, the people, and the ways of the folks of the southside because he grew up there. He told me he always endeavored to treat people the same, no matter their skin color, no matter what side of town they were from, nor what side of town they were in at the moment.

Because I asked, he shared one story of a newly-hired White cop on the beat who was going to be his riding partner for an evening shift. As the evening began, the rookie cop asked Tommey if they could go over to the southside (the Flats) so he could arrest somebody, as he thought that would look good on his record as a new policeman. Tommey agreed to go over there but told the rookie to lay low and learn from what he was about to see and experience. Sure enough, it was easy to spot an arrest if so desired — a drunk man loitering the streets like so many did any night of the week. The new cop wanted to arrest the drunkard right on the spot. Tommey told him to stay in the squad car and to observe how he handled the situation... the rookie might learn something. Tommey knew the man personally and knew he'd been going through some difficult times. He told him he shouldn't be out and around when he gets that way and told him to give him the keys to his car, and

Officer Tommey Morris

he would take him home. The man complied, and Tommey and the rookie put him in the back seat of the squad car and drove him to his house. Tommey knocked on the man's house with keys in hand to give to the wife. He did and they put the man to bed to sleep it off. The wife was embarrassed but appreciative. Years later, this man came up to Tommey and told him he'd gotten his life together and appreciated greatly how Tommey had not arrested him but helped him, and he was grateful. Those kinds of stories abound all around the southside about Tommey Morris ... a hundred-fold. Or is it two or three?

By the time I met Tommey, he'd been retired from the police force for thirteen years. Yet people still know Tommey Morris. I felt honored that he agreed to chauffeur me around the Black community in his big ol' black 2011 Chevy pickup and show me things I knew not of (as mentioned earlier, I was back in town gathering information about the long-forgotten and unacknowl-edged history of Odessa's The Velvets who got their start at Blackshear High School in 1960). By this time, I hadn't lived in Odessa since 1968, but it most likely would not have mattered ... I still would have been ignorant of what I learned the day Tommey took me around. Oh my — the things I learned.

There was the Harlem movie theater (affectionately known as "The Colored Show"), where back in Tommey's day one could get in for nine cents, and with a quarter still have money left over for a Coke or Snickers. The brick-walled theater is all dilapidated now and has been vacant for decades. It was about the size of an elongated two-car garage. But those walls still hold memories, good memories for the old timers who had good times there. By seeing this, I was getting a glimpse of the kind of life these folks led — separate, but unequal. He showed me the Texas State Historical Marker at The Penny House where Black travelers in the 1940s through the early '60s would stay when passing through Odessa (hotel accommodations across the tracks were off limits to people of color). He took me by the old shuttered, dinky, skating rink, and the small teen club known as The Blue Front, where Black kids would go for dancing and soda pops ... We drove passed the boarded-up iconic Doc Bracy's lunch spot, where folks lined up to get one of Doc's famous "half weenie hotdogs" piled high with his special chili ... a bright spot for kids of all ages on the southside. We slowly cruised by the former campus grounds of Blackshear Junior/Senior High, where it's been repurposed as Blackshear Magnet Elementary School. Memories ... I could tell Tommey was reliving some of those as he was chauffeuring me around. We passed by the barren dusty football field where Tommey once ran for touchdowns. He drove me around the area known as the Flats where the night clubs once filled the night air with honky tonk music and whiffs of Jack Daniels or Wild Turkey. Then there was Miss Whitiker's house, where the ninety-three years-young matriarch of the Black community still lives. We went by his church where the faith and values he espouses were taught and reinforced. He pointed out where Dr. Wheatley Stewart once had his house that served as a medical clinic for Black patients. Only in emergencies could Dr. Stewart/ Black folks use the big new hospital across town (where I was born in 1950) ... if surgery was required, Dr. Stewart was allowed to use the hospital *basement* for the procedure. Decades later, and in recognition of Dr. Wheatley's contribution to the life and culture of the Odessa community, that hospital now has a pavilion area named after Dr. Wheatley Stewart in his honor — my, how times have changed. For the good this time.

While Tommey was giving me the tour of his old haunts, I was beginning to feel embarrassed by my own igno-rance. I was just too young and naïve to know much of this stuff. Like so many others, I had just lived my life on the other side of the tracks and had no need to know of or care about this whole 'nother world just a couple miles from my house over on Bernice Street. But I quickly was growing to admire and respect my driver and new friend Tommey. Never did I detect any bitter feelings for his lot in life. He had better ways of thinking. I could tell he was having good thoughts toward me as well ... the one who had privileges he did not have, and that I had taken for granted.

"I love you, man."
"Me, too."

Tommey's been a church-goer most his life and a true believer in the One who made us all. A man of deep personal faith. Not perfect, mind you ... Tommey's made his mistakes alright and got his regrets and shortcomings as we all do. Told me so. That just made him more real and genuine to me. Wife Vina and Tommey just celebrated their Fiftieth wedding anniversary in May. What an example that is — sticking together in the hard times as well as the good.

We connected as brothers that beautiful day, Tommey and me. As I was writing my book, I had opportunity to have numerous encounters with him over those couple of years. He grew to embrace my quirky sense of humor.

Tommy exhorted his "Little Buddy" to set his goals high and never give up.

Like when we'd be having lunch together, I'd sometimes blurt out to the waiter something like: "You know who this guy is? This is Tommey "the Twister" Morris! Famous athlete from the southside from back in the day. Before you were ever born, or were even thought about, young fella! You ought to get his autograph. Could be worth something someday, you know." Tommey would just sit there probably feeling a little proud and a little embarrassed at the same time. Then I'd follow-up to the waiter with something like: "Truth be known — Mr. Tommey here was *also* the all-time 'champeen tiddlywinks' player in school history. Just saying ... "

I think one of the most enduring character qualities Tommey has is his humility. When accolades or praise might come his way, he just naturally deflects those sentiments toward others. He'd say things to me like, "Charlie, I got all that stuff in school. I don't need any more. I want all those type thoughts or gestures or words go to others that might need any encouragement this day." What kind of person does that? I know ... a self-effacing, genuinely kind person. I know a handful of people like that. I always feel a little better being around them — hoping it might rub off on me, no matter hue of skin. Tommey was a *police officer* alright ... but after knowing him, I'd say *peace officer* is the more perfect moniker.

*"Blessed are the peacemakers for they shall be called the children of God." Matthew 5:9*

*Tommey James Morris Sr. entered the gates of eternal peace on September 16, 2023.*

# ACKNOWLEDGMENTS

There are several people I'd like to acknowledge and thank for making *Remembrances II* a reality. First, it would be my wife, Carolyn. She's been my go-to person with any computer/printing/scanning-related issues. She's helped me gather many of the pictures herein, has been my sounding board for any corny story ideas, and has been an initial proofreader on most of the narratives. She's also *in* the book, so she's lived some of these with me. Thank you, sweet Carolyn, for being there when I needed another perspective in the writings ... *and* finding lost pics/items in the Norman computer abyss.

I'd like to thank my local editor, Connie Parr, for her input, expertise, time, and counsel in putting together a cohesive manuscript. She made things a lot smoother, and I appreciate her insights in helping me with the nuances of saying things in just the right way to better connect with the reader. Her availability, upbeat and accommodating manner, and ability to find ways to make things work were significant to the project.

I thank Janie Jessee, my publisher and owner of Jan-Carol Publishing — for believing in me and feeling that my stories are worthy of publication. I appreciate her greatly (as well as Draco, Tara, and all the JCP staff). Because of these professionals, hopefully many folks can enjoy a respite from the busyness of our world and read something that will entertain, challenge, or inspire them as they go through the stories.

Finally, little could I imagine that a 2015 *Providential* encounter with a lady at a local lunch spot in Blountville, Tennessee, would have a far-reaching impact in my life. Susan Tanner and I were just two people interested in ancestral genealogies at the time ... we got to talking, had several things in common, became friends, and I sent her some of my original short stories for fun. She *really* liked them and strongly suggested that I seek a wider audience by submitting some of my articles to *Good Old Days Magazine* and later Jan-Carol Publishing. I did, and three books later, here we are! My sincere gratitude goes to my dear Tennessee friend, Susan, for her initiative, encouragement, and friendship. I'm gonna keep on writing as the Good Lord gives me days and ideas to do just that.

# ABOUT THE AUTHOR

PHOTO BY NOELLE NORMAN OVERTURF

Charlie Norman has been writing stories since his days long ago as editor of his high school newspaper in the late 1960s. That flair for writing lay dormant for decades as he pursued a career in the airline industry until retirement in 2010. But he was always a story teller and over the years had some wonderfully unique experiences and met some intriguing people that made their tale worth telling. Enough so that these stories are now compiled in this new book *REMEMBRANCES II*, the follow-up to his first *REMEMBRANCES* (published by Jan-Carol Publishing in 2021). Charlie also documented in book form the fascinating story of the early 1960s nationally known "Doo-Wop" singing group *The Velvets*, and his relationship with the bass singer of the group from their old hometown of Odessa, Texas. This encounter and narrative lead to his book: *ROAD TO RECONCILIATION ... AND BEYOND Unlikely Friends Become Brothers* (2022). Charlie and his wife Carolyn make their home in the country in rural north central Texas, have two adult children, five terrific grandsons, and one wonderfully-spoiled granddaughter.

Printed in the USA
CPSIA information can be obtained
at www.ICGtesting.com
LVHW020557020524
778879LV00018B/1238